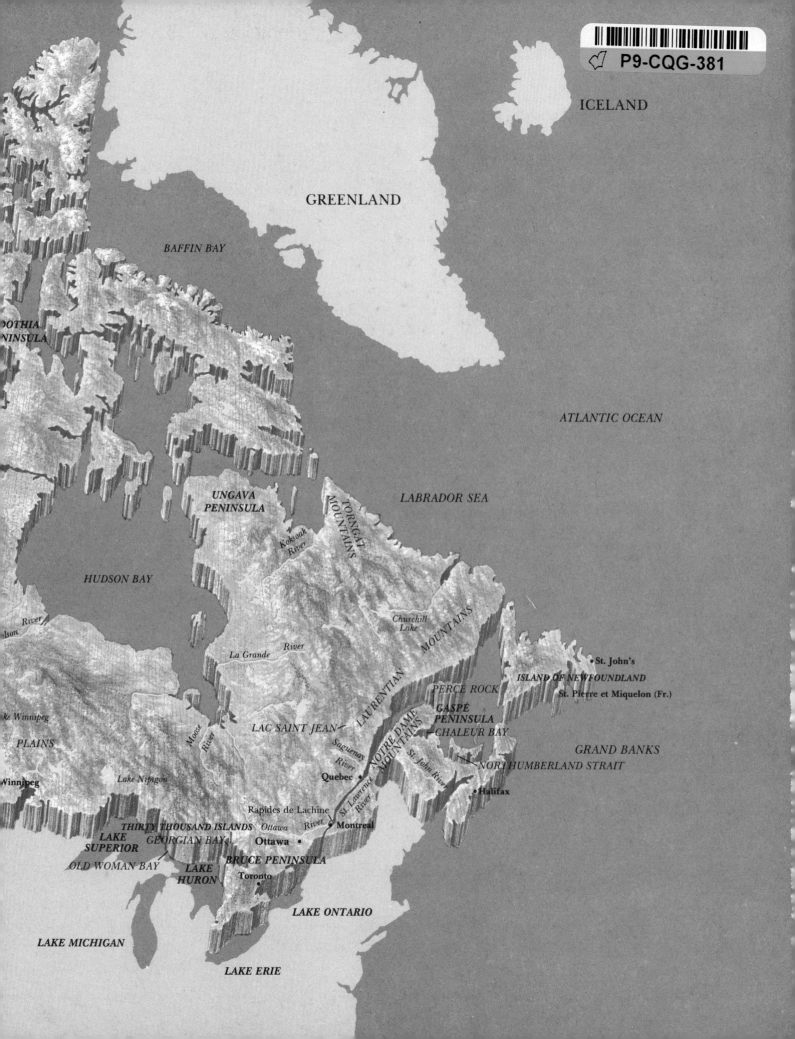

ICELAND

GREENLAND

BAFFIN BAY

OOTHIA
NINSULA

ATLANTIC OCEAN

LABRADOR SEA

UNGAVA
PENINSULA

Koksoak
River

TORNGAT
MOUNTAINS

HUDSON BAY

Churchill
Lake

MOUNTAINS

River

La Grande   River

St. John's

ISLAND OF NEWFOUNDLAND

St. Pierre et Miquelon (Fr.)

PERCÉ ROCK

LAURENTIAN

GASPÉ
PENINSULA

GRAND BANKS

lson   River

LAC SAINT JEAN

NOTRE DAME
MOUNTAINS

CHALEUR BAY

ke Winnipeg

Moose
River

Saguenay
River

St. John River

NORTHUMBERLAND STRAIT

PLAINS

Lake Nipigon

Quebec

Winnipeg

Rapides de Lachine

St. Lawrence River

Halifax

THIRTY THOUSAND ISLANDS

Ottawa   River

Montreal

GEORGIAN BAY

Ottawa

LAKE
SUPERIOR

OLD WOMAN BAY

BRUCE PENINSULA

LAKE
HURON

Toronto

LAKE ONTARIO

LAKE MICHIGAN

LAKE ERIE

CANADA

CANADA

By the Editors of Time-Life Books

TIME-LIFE BOOKS ∘ ALEXANDRIA, VIRGINIA

TIME® LIFE BOOKS

Cover: Bundles of straw gathered by a baler
dot a recently harvested wheat field near the
town of Douglas in western Manitoba.

Time-Life Books Inc.
is a wholly owned subsidiary of

TIME INCORPORATED

FOUNDER: HENRY R. LUCE 1898-1967

Editor-in-Chief: Jason McManus
Chairman and Chief Executive Officer: J. Richard Munro
President and Chief Operating Officer: N. J. Nicholas Jr.
Editorial Director: Ray Cave
Executive Vice President, Books: Kelso F. Sutton
Vice President, Books: George Artandi

TIME-LIFE BOOKS INC.

EUROPEAN EDITOR: Kit van Tulleken
Assistant European Editor: Gillian Moore
Design Director: Ed Skyner
Chief of Research: Vanessa Kramer
Chief Sub-editor: Ilse Gray

LIBRARY OF NATIONS

Editorial Staff for *Canada*
Editor: Tony Allan
Researcher: Anton Neumann
Designer: Lynne Brown
Picture Editors: Christine Hinze (principal),
Mark Karras
Sub-editor: Wendy Gibbons
Picture Coordinator: Peggy Tout
Editorial Assistant: Molly Oates

EDITORIAL PRODUCTION

Coordinator: Nikki Allen
Assistant: Maureen Kelly
Editorial Department: Theresa John, Debra Lelliott

Special Contributors: The chapter texts were written by
Windsor Chorlton, John Fraser, Frederic V. Grun-
feld, Alan Lothian, and Mel Watkins.

Other contributors: Michael Ignatieff and
Christopher Maynard.

Assistant Editor for the U.S. edition: Barbara Fairchild
Quarmby

Front and back endpapers: A topographic map
showing the major rivers, lakes, mountain
ranges, and other natural features of Canada
appears on the front endpaper; the back
endpaper shows the 10 provinces and two
territories that make up the nation, together
with a selection of the principal towns.

CONSULTANTS

Michael Ignatieff is a Canadian writer
and broadcaster now living in London.
His recent work includes a philosophical
essay entitled *The Needs of Strangers,* and
The Russian Album.

Donald H. Simpson is the librarian of the
Royal Commonwealth Society and a
former president of the British Association for Canadian Studies.

First Printing

Printed in U.S.A.
Published simultaneously in Canada.
School and library distribution by Silver Burdett
Company, Morristown, New Jersey.

TIME-LIFE is a trademark of Time Incorporated
U.S.A.

Library of Congress Cataloging in Publication Data
Canada.
   (Library of nations)
   Bibliography: p.
   Includes index.
   1. Canada I. Time-Life Books. II. Series.
F1008.C313 1988   971   87-33641
ISBN 0-8094-5148-4
ISBN 0-8094-5149-2 (lib. bdg.)

CONTENTS

Contained within a giant boom, a floating island of logs drifts downstream to a sawmill in Quebec. Canada's lakes and rivers, which form natural

AN EVERGREEN RESOURCE

- BOREAL FOREST
- MOUNTAIN FOREST
- MIXED FOREST/FARMLAND
- FARMLAND
- MIXED FOREST/TUNDRA
- TUNDRA
- GRASSLAND

Sandwiched between tundra to the north and grassland to the south-west, the unbroken belt of forest that covers 48 percent of Canada constitutes the country's most distinctive landscape feature and its greatest renewable resource. About 75 percent of Canada's productive woodland is boreal forest, dominated by the cold-tolerant spruce, bal-sam fir, and pine; but British Columbia's mountain forest, character-ized by cedar and hemlock as well as fir, yields the richest harvest—half of all the wood cut in Canada from one seventh of its forested land. Although only 1 percent of Canadians are directly employed in forestry, about 1 job in 10 is dependent on the lumber, paper, and other wood-using industries that accounted for slightly more than 14 percent of the nation's commodity exports in 1986.

highways leading to the heart of the country, still provide a cheap and efficient means of transporting lumber from wilderness regions.

An intrepid crew steers its inflatable raft through rapids at Garvin's Shoot on the Ottawa River. In a country with 30,000 lakes larger than three

square miles, countless small lakes, and many rivers, boating is a national passion, and many Canadian families own some kind of craft.

A CHANGING PATTERN OF TRADE

As a country of vast resources and small population, Canada has always relied on trade for its economic well-being. Today, it ranks among the world's top-10 trading nations, and the value of its exports—ranging from aircraft and communications satellites to wheat and zinc—helps Canadians maintain a standard of living that is among the highest in the world. About half of the goods produced in Canada are exported, making it one of fewer than six countries that export more than they import.

Until World War II, Canada's trade was dominated by its relationship with Britain, which bought 40 percent of the country's exports. Today, Canada's economic health, including the value of the Canadian dollar, is linked to that of the United States, which in 1985 took 75 percent of Canada's exports and supplied 72 percent of its imports.

American companies also have a controlling interest in many sectors of the economy, but the steady growth of Canadian capital—much of it accumulated from investment in the United States—has reduced fears of foreign domination.

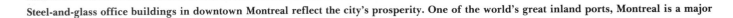

Steel-and-glass office buildings in downtown Montreal reflect the city's prosperity. One of the world's great inland ports, Montreal is a major

10

transportation center for the exports that underpin the Canadian economy, as well as being an important manufacturing city in its own right.

LINKS ACROSS A CONTINENT

TRANS-CANADA HIGHWAY ——

ALASKA HIGHWAY ——

CANADIAN PACIFIC RAILWAY ——

CANADIAN NATIONAL RAILWAYS ― ―

Canada's transportation network has been shaped by the distribution of the country's population, concentrated in a transcontinental corridor above the U.S. border. Integrating the settlements within this belt has been a major task for Canadians, who literally forged national unity with the construction of the 4,375-mile-long Canadian Pacific Railway. Completed in 1885, the CPR provided the main east-west land link until the Trans-Canada Highway was completed in 1970.

A Canadian Pacific freight train threads its way through Kicking Horse Pass in the Canadian Rockies. The 5,330-foot pass, the highest point on the

...anscontinental railway, is also used by the Trans-Canada Highway.

Smoke from a smelter drifts over mountains of ore at a nickel mine in Ontario's Sudbury Basin, whose mineral wealth was accidentally discovered in

THE UNDERGROUND WEALTH OF A NATION

Few countries are as rich in minerals as Canada. The mining industry is not only represented in almost every region but boasts the world's most diverse output—more than 60 different mineral types. In total mineral production, Canada is third after the United States and the U.S.S.R., and it ranks first in the extraction of zinc, uranium, and ilmenite, the major source of titanium. It is also the world's largest exporter of minerals, selling about 80 percent abroad—although its oil and gas fields are exploited only for internal consumption.

Mining contributes more than 10 percent of Canada's gross national product and employs 6 percent of the work force, but the exploitation of the country's natural wealth also has negative aspects. Airborne pollution from smelter chimneys has contaminated many lakes and rivers, while some wilderness areas have been disfigured by large-scale mining developments.

	VALUE IN C$ MILLION*	% OF WORLD PRODUCTION	RANK AMONG PRODUCER NATIONS
CRUDE PETROLEUM	17,615	3%	8th
NATURAL GAS	7,641	5%	3rd
IRON ORE	1,433	5%	5th
COPPER	1,392	8%	4th
ZINC	1,316	18%	1st
GOLD	1,227	6%	3rd
NICKEL	1,061	22%	2nd
URANIUM	842	25%	1st
POTASH	718	26%	2nd
SILVER	448	10%	5th
ASBESTOS	374	20%	2nd
ILMENITE	108	21%	1st

*AVERAGED FIGURES FOR 1983-1985.

1883 by workers blasting a route for the Canadian Pacific Railway. Today, half a dozen different metals are mined in the vicinity.

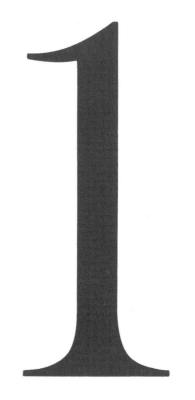

In the depths of winter, snow blankets a residential area of Montreal, Canada's second-largest city. Situated on an island in the St. Lawrence, Montreal gets an average of 18 inches of snow per month from December to March, when the mean temperature is between 25° F. and 10° F.

THE GIANT OF THE NORTH

One of Canada's prime ministers, William Lyon Mackenzie King, once remarked that while some countries have too much history, Canada has too much geography. With a land area of nearly four million square miles, Canada covers 7 percent of the earth's surface; of all the world's nations, only the Soviet Union is bigger. From Lake Erie in the south to its northernmost extremity on the Arctic Ocean, it measures 3,000 miles. From east to west, Canada spans more than 3,125 miles, putting the city of Vancouver, located on its Pacific coast, closer to Mexico City in Central America than to Halifax, on the nation's Atlantic seaboard.

The natural features of this land are likewise magnified on a prodigious scale. Canada has two million lakes, more than half the world's total, containing 50 percent of all the fresh water on earth. It has 18 islands that exceed 4,000 square miles in area, including Baffin, which is almost as large as France, and Ellesmere, which has a glacier that is nearly twice the size of Switzerland. Its prairies alone cover more than the combined areas of India, Pakistan, and Nepal.

Much of this great land is still a wilderness, however, inhabited by wild beasts and silence. It is a northern expanse of tundra and boreal forest, glaciated mountain peaks, and plunging fjords—a landscape shaped by ice. Only 18,000 years ago, Canada was the center of an ice sheet as large as Antarctica; and even today, 50 percent of its territory lies within zones of permafrost, where the ground has been frozen to a depth of up to 1,313 feet by thousands of years of winter temperatures that fall as low as $-76°$ F.

But it is not just the arctic regions that are crippled by seasonal cold. Canada's climate is of the extreme continental type, characterized by scorching summers and long winters, when wave after wave of polar air pushes the temperature below freezing in every part of the country except the extreme southwest. In fact, although the cities of Toronto, Ottawa, and Montreal lie in the same latitude as Bordeaux, the French Riviera, and Florence, they experience bitter winters in which the temperature may fall below $32°$ F. for more than 150 days each year.

The severity of Canada's weather means that only 12 percent of the land is suitable for farming, but that extent of Canada—concentrated mainly in the prairies of the west—is equivalent to the combined areas of France, Italy, West Germany, and England, and is sufficient to make the nation one of the world's granaries. The other 88 percent has proved to be a treasure trove of natural resources—fish, furs, timber, and minerals, each of which in turn has helped lay the foundations of an economic empire. Canada is still primarily an exporter of its resources. Ranked ninth among the trading nations in the early 1980s, Canada was the

1

world's leading supplier of newsprint, nickel, silver, barley, wheat, and fish. The sale of primary products such as these, rather than the vigor of the country's manufacturing industries, has helped give Canadians the world's third-highest standard of living, after Switzerland and the United States.

Yet for all its size and wealth, Canada had only 25.3 million inhabitants in the mid-1980s, giving a population density of little more than five people for every square mile—12 times less than the figure for the neighboring United States and one hundredth that of crowded Great Britain or of West Germany. But even this does not convey a true picture of the country's lonely expanses, since most Canadians live within 200 miles of the U.S. border while four fifths of the country has never been settled permanently. The northern void has always held a fascination for Canadians, and

the theme of the small communities defending themselves from an overwhelming solitude is central to Canada's history and literature.

Although less valid today, when nearly 3 out of 4 Canadians live in towns and cities—a higher proportion than in the United States—the feeling of exposure to an immense and hostile environment is preserved in the Canadian psyche. The country's immense spaces exhilarate, but they can also oppress, awakening doubts that a nation occupying so little deserves to own so much. "My God, is all this ours!" exclaims a character in Hugh MacLennan's *Two Solitudes,* one of the first novels to explore the problem of Canadian national identity.

To foreigners, Canada may seem so large as to be invisible. That is partly because the nation has never aspired to the position of a leading world power.

Although Canada belongs to all the major global organizations and has the distinction of being the only country in the world to have participated in every one of the peace-keeping missions undertaken by the United Nations since World War II, Canada commands surprisingly little international attention. "In the newspapers of continental Europe," the Canadian writer Richard Gwyn has pointed out, "Iceland could give Canada a close contest for column inches."

Perhaps the lack of media coverage given to Canadian affairs stems from the country's proximity to the United States, with which it shares not only a border but—for many of its citizens—a common European heritage, language, and economic system. Although its political philosophy and foreign policy differ from the United States', Canada is hard-pressed to project its own national identity as different from that of its economically powerful and culturally assertive neighbor. For Canadians, the problem is compounded by the fact that they cannot agree on what that identity is—although they are pretty sure what it is not.

To begin with, Canada is not a homogenous nation. The basic division in its society is between the 40 percent of the population who are of English-speaking parentage and the 30 percent who are French by origin. Most of the Anglophones are the descendants of groups who settled in Canada after 1763, when the country became a British colony. The distinctive French Canadian culture results from the perseverance of the country's original colonists—the French fur trappers and traders who were the principal inhabitants of the land before the British

18

victory—for there has been virtually no renewal of immigration from France since that date.

The remaining 30 percent of the population comprises immigrants from continental Europe, with Germans, who number more than one million, forming the largest group. There are also more than half a million Canadians of Italian origin; a similar number from the Ukraine; more than a quarter of a million each from Poland, Scandinavia, and the Netherlands; and about 100,000 from China, Greece, and Hungary; as well as sizable populations of Yugoslavian, Korean, Portuguese, West Indian, and Russian descent. Native Indians and Inuit (Eskimo), who had the country to themselves until the French established the first permanent European settlement in 1605, accounted for less than 1 percent of the population in the mid-1980s.

The historical divergences of economic interests and culture among the colonial settlers ensured that Canada adopted a hybrid political structure when it achieved nationhood in 1867. From Britain, Canada inherited a system of parliamentary democracy and a constitutional monarchy, with the British sovereign remaining as head of state but exercising only nominal power. The sheer vastness of the country, however, and the mutual antagonism that existed between the French- and English-speakers ensured that Canada, against all the intentions of its founding fathers, would also become a decentralized federal state. The nation consisted at the time of four semiautonomous provinces—Nova Scotia, New Brunswick, Quebec, and Ontario—which were united in "one Dominion under the name of Canada." Since then, the federation has been enlarged by the ad-

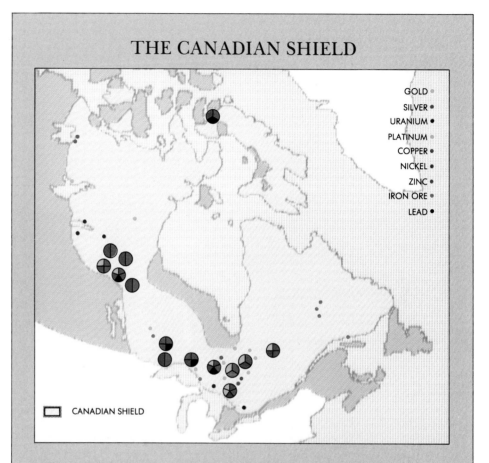

THE CANADIAN SHIELD

GOLD
SILVER
URANIUM
PLATINUM
COPPER
NICKEL
ZINC
IRON ORE
LEAD

CANADIAN SHIELD

When explorer Jacques Cartier became the first European to view the coast of Labrador in 1534, its bleakness prompted him to dub it "the land God gave to Cain." The name has since been applied to the geophysical region called the Canadian Shield, of which Labrador is the easternmost part. Forming a horseshoe around Hudson Bay, the Shield—a granite plateau rising to some 6,200 feet above sea level—covers 1.8 million square

miles, nearly half the country.

It is one of the world's oldest landscapes, its surface rocks dating back 600 million years. Eons of erosion, especially by Ice Age glaciers, have stripped most of its soil, except in boggy lowlands. Elsewhere, stretches of forest alternate with innumerable lakes and rivers. Human settlements are few and are concentrated near mineral deposits of gold, silver, and nickel—the hidden wealth of the Shield.

1

dition of Manitoba, British Columbia, Prince Edward Island, Saskatchewan, Alberta, and Newfoundland, a latecomer that joined the federation only in 1949. Completing the political map of Canada are the Yukon Territory and the Northwest Territories—huge, sparsely populated northern tracts that fall under the direct jurisdiction of the federal government in Ottawa.

By contrast, each of the 10 provinces is largely self-governing, with its own miniature parliamentary system, premier, cabinet, and legislative assembly. While the federal government deals with matters of national and international importance, the provincial governments have, to a degree that can astonish foreigners, a wide measure of autonomy over such matters as natural resources, education, health, and law. Each province has the right to maintain legations in foreign countries; at least one of them—French-speaking Quebec—has effectively been operating a foreign policy of its own choosing, in terms of cultural and linguistic ties if not of defense.

Canada's federal structure has created an increase in provincial loyalties, although a strong sense of separatism has developed in Quebec. The system recognizes the fact that the provinces, far from being neatly matched parts of a uniform country, are small commonwealths. Each has its own physical and

A laker built to travel the shallow waters of the St. Lawrence Seaway-Great Lakes Waterway negotiates one of eight locks on the Welland Ship Canal linking Lakes Erie and Ontario. The 27-mile-long canal, bypassing the turbulent Niagara River, lifts vessels almost 330 feet in its locks.

cultural identities; each has its own peoples, with different outlooks and lifestyles; and each has its own resources and needs. Because regional loyalties have for a long time vied with the national voice in the hearts of Canadians, the sense of a pan-Canadian identity has remained low-key.

The differences and rivalries among the provinces are the more striking because the provincial boundaries are not natural divisions but arbitrary lines produced by surveyors and the compromises of politicians. The three Prairie Provinces, for example, are laid out with the precision of city blocks on one of the most undifferentiated landscapes to be found, yet their inhabitants cherish their separate identities. Increasingly, these identities owe less to cultural and ethnic origins than to different standards of living, which are jealously guarded, sometimes by protectionist policies. A provincial government may, for instance, insist on subletting government contracts to local firms even in the face of a number of lower bids from outside competitors; or it may demand that all employers in a given industry use only resident labor.

At the same time, many of Canada's provinces are so large that disparities within them can be great. In terms of life-style, a French Canadian businessman in Montreal has little in common with his fellow-Quebecois who works as a logger in a remote forest settlement 312.5 miles to the north.

In fact, Canada falls naturally into six great geographical regions, whose boundaries only accidentally coincide with those of the provinces. The most southerly, and the most densely populated, is the Great Lakes-St. Lawrence Lowlands, a narrow corridor running

2,500 miles from Lake Superior in the west to the Gulf of St. Lawrence in the east, covering both southern Ontario and southern Quebec. To the east, the Appalachian Mountains have been ground down by ice and carved by the sea into islands and peninsulas that delineate the coastal world of the four Atlantic, or Maritime, Provinces: Nova Scotia, New Brunswick, Prince Edward Island, and Newfoundland. To the north lies the vast Canadian Shield, a wilderness of lake, forest, and tundra that covers Labrador (the mainland part of Newfoundland), northern Quebec and Ontario, and much of the Northwest Territories; it also covers half of Manitoba and cuts corners off Saskatchewan and Alberta. The greater part of these last three provinces, however, falls within the Great Plains, or Prairies region, a 1,000-mile swath of flat grassland that stretches west as

far as the fifth region, the Western Cordillera. This great mountain complex extends 1,250 miles from the 49th parallel to the Alaskan border, taking in the province of British Columbia and a large part of the Yukon Territory. The rest of the Yukon Territory and Northwest Territories, including the great icy islands of the Canadian Arctic, constitute the nation's final region, the Far North.

With so much space available to them, fully 60 percent of Canadians have elected to live in the 5 percent of their territory taken up by the Great Lakes-St. Lawrence Lowlands. There is a historical logic in their choice, for the nation of Canada originally developed along this axis, which drew trappers and traders steadily westward into the unexplored interior of the country. Most of the nation's inhabitants now live within an easy day's drive of the

21

1

Three generations of a family relax at Lake Kingsmere, in Gatineau Provincial Park, just north of Ottawa. Canada's major cities have more unspoiled countryside around them than those of almost any other nation, and the Friday-evening escape from town of the wealthy is an urban phenomenon.

Canada-U.S. border, where it is deflected from its arrow-straight course along the 49th parallel by the five lakes—Superior, Michigan, Huron, Erie, and Ontario—that the St. Lawrence drains. First traveled by the canoe-borne fur trappers known as *voyageurs* in the 16th century, the lakes are now navigated by great grain and ore carriers that are able to penetrate inland as far west as the piers and silos of Thunder Bay on the farther shore of Lake Superior. The port, formed by the merger of Port Arthur and Fort William in 1970, is the principal railhead for prairie wheat and boasts the world's largest grain-handling facility. Until the early-19th century, however, Thunder Bay was preeminent as a rendezvous for trappers and the depot from which the fur traders of the North West Company sent their fleets of canoes toward the prairies and mountains of the west.

Between Thunder Bay and Lake Huron, the only large town is Sault Ste. Marie, a major steel producer that also maintains the world's largest fleet of planes for fighting forest fires. Glowing with their own radiance during the brief autumn season, the forests of southern Ontario provide a natural divide between the population centers to the east of the Great Lakes and the Prairie Provinces beyond.

At one point, north of Lake Huron's Georgian Bay, however, the sylvan landscape is interrupted by a satanic vision of fiery slag heaps and blighted vegetation. This is Sudbury, Canada's most important mining community, whose position as the world's largest single producer of nickel is commemorated by a 33-foot-tall model of a Canadian five-cent piece (made, in this case, of stainless steel). In the 1960s, the pitted landscape left by the extraction

of the metal was so desolate that it was used as a training ground for American astronauts preparing themselves for landings on the moon. Although the area became the site of a land reclamation project in the following decade, at the beginning of the 1980s, one of Sudbury's smelters still had the dubious distinction of emitting more of the noxious sulfur dioxide alleged to be the principal ingredient of acid rain than any other offender in the Americas. Canadians, however, are emphatic in their denunciation of industries in the United States, which they believe are the source of more than half the pollution that threatens their forests.

South of Sudbury, the road to Toronto passes through steadily more populous and cultivated country, with the forests broken by neat orchards and dairy farms and small Victorian brick towns. The forest is always in the background, however—a threatening and morbid presence in the winter, when the blood-red sun struggles to clear the treetops; but it becomes a source of renewal in the summer, when it is invaded by an army of vacationers including fishermen, sun-worshipers, hikers, canoeists and many other wilderness lovers. "The cottage"—as Canadians call their summer houses where they get on familiar terms with nature—is, together with ice hockey, the country's great cross-cultural institution. Only 6 percent of families own a cottage, but many more would like to.

Come winter, which has generally set in by the end of November, all but the skiers have returned to the cities. For nearly three million Canadians, home is Toronto, the provincial capital of Ontario, the country's largest metropolitan area, and its financial and commercial center. Dominated by the twin

22

On the eastern shore of Ontario's Georgian Bay, a cluster of islets, reefs, and outcrops forming part of the Thirty Thousand Islands archipelago provide sites for dozens of vacation homes. Called cottages, these part-time residences are often large and luxuriously furnished.

symbols of its ascendancy, the 1,800-foot-tall CN (Canadian National) Tower and the Royal Bank Plaza, Toronto spreads from a flat, downtown section fronting Lake Ontario to sprawling suburbs set in gently rolling hills. Most of the city is laid out on a rectangular grid plan, which is interrupted by a green belt of wooded parkland created by two small rivers.

Until the 1950s, the social tone of Toronto was as rigid and uncompromising as its street plan. The city was established by staunchly British settlers and by Empire Loyalists—pro-British refugees who fled northward from the fledgling United States after the War of Independence. Toronto's citizens nourished bitter memories of the War of 1812, when American troops destroyed the town's parliament buildings. (The British responded to this by burning Washington's government buildings and the presidential mansion.) From its founders, Toronto inherited resolutely anti-American, anti-Catholic, and anti-French-Canadian instincts. Its political attitudes shocked the visiting English novelist Charles Dickens: "The wild and rabid Toryism of Toronto is, I speak seriously, *appalling*," he wrote to a friend. Puritanical to a fault, the city fathers made sure that everything but the churches remained closed on Sunday; the main department store drew curtains over its displays to deny passersby the pleasure of window-shopping. While on a visit to Toronto in 1913, the English poet Rupert Brooke damned the city with faint praise. "It is all right," he wrote. "The only depressing thing is that it will always be what it is, only larger."

Brooke was right about Toronto's growing larger, but he was wrong about its inability to change. What trans-

Rising behind skyscrapers in the heart of Toronto, the mast of the CN Tower, the world's tallest free-standing structure, soars to more than 1,800 feet. Built in the 1970s as a communications center, the CN Tower also houses a revolving restaurant and observation decks.

formed the city was an enormous post-war influx of immigrants from continental Europe, who now make up one third of the population. With more than 80,000 Greeks and 300,000 Italians, as well as Ukrainians, Portuguese, Chinese, Hungarians, and other ethnic communities, Toronto has become a much spicier mix of cultures; each has its own distinctive neighborhood, markets, and entertainments. And the city has also managed to retain its reputation as "Toronto the Good"—a pleasant and clean urban environment whose streets are safe to walk alone at night.

In Toronto's hinterland, the town names read like a list from a gazetteer of Great Britain—Durham, Exeter, and Newmarket rub shoulders with Paisley, Cambridge, and Stratford, which holds its own annual Shakespeare festival. Occasionally, a name such as New Hamburg or New Prussia intrudes to show that this fertile corner of Canada was also favored by German settlers. Many Germans, together with Mennonites from Pennsylvania, put down roots in the city formerly known as Berlin, which is now the manufacturing center around Kitchener and Waterloo, whose splendidly British imperial name rests uneasily on a place that celebrates its origins with an annual Oktoberfest.

Between Toronto and Montreal there are 337.5 miles of highway and a keen, sometimes acrid, rivalry that is mediated by the strategic position of Ottawa, the federal capital, roughly midway between the two. Originally called Bytown, the city was rechristened Ottawa in 1855. (The name comes from a local Indian tribe.) Two years later, Queen Victoria, tired of the rival claims of Toronto and Montreal, chose Ottawa as the compromise candidate for Canada's seat of government. Work on the Victorian Gothic pinnacles of the Canadian Parliament buildings started two years after that, on a clifftop site overlooking a river jammed by the log booms of American timber barons. One journalist of the day referred to Ottawa unflatteringly as "a sub-Arctic lumber village converted by royal mandate into a political cockpit."

Today, with a population of about 700,000 inhabitants, extensive parks, and an opera house, theater, and studio housed in the National Arts Center, Ottawa is a pleasant place to live in and to visit. However, like other artificially created capitals such as Canberra or Brasilia, Ottawa is not calculated to quicken significantly the pulse of any but those who live for and by politics.

Montreal, less than 120 miles to the east but a whole culture apart, is a much headier place. The largest city in Quebec and the most populous in Canada until overtaken by Toronto in 1985, it still has more French-speaking citizens than any city except Paris. No less a figure than General Charles de Gaulle once described it as France's second city, to the consternation of other Canadians. Although large minorities of Scots, Irish, continental Europeans,

On the frozen Rideau Canal in Ottawa, ice skaters pass beneath the Mackenzie King Bridge. Beyond the bridge on the left, the modern National Arts Center and the neo-Gothic Parliament buildings face the Government Conference Center and the turreted Chateau Laurier Hotel.

1

Chinese, and West Indians have now made Montreal the most cosmopolitan metropolis in the country, its tone remains resolutely French. Indeed, in 1975, a bill was passed that required all children of immigrants whose native language was not English to learn French. The law was extended in 1977; since then, all newcomers to Quebec have had to send their children to French-language schools. This legislation had the effect of defusing much of the separatist anger that had shaken the province in the 1960s and early years of the 1970s.

Montreal has always been a turbulent place, prone to linguistic and political shifts of fortune. In 1760, when the city capitulated to the British after the fall of Quebec, the population of 5,000 was wholly French. By 1830, the balance of French- and English-speakers was roughly equal, and although the French regained numerical dominance in the 1860s, the commercial life of the city, by then a great port, remained largely in British hands. Scots businessmen prospered. They celebrated their affluence by constructing vast granite-and-sandstone mansions, replete with grand crenellations and arrow-slit windows. The style was christened by local wags as Highland Flaunt-It. The Scots chose to dominate the heights of the city as well as the heights of the economy. The higher up the hill they built, the better the address; and the better the address, the more likely the street was called McGregor, Redpath, or Mc-Tavish. But as the city's prosperity increased, so did its reputation for wickedness. The high moral tone of its Presbyterian upper class housed on the slopes of exclusive Mount Royal contrasted with prostitution, illegal gambling, and gangsterism downtown; yet all managed to flourish under the venal eye of the city's civic authorities.

The situation was ameliorated by Jean Drapeau, a city official whose war on corruption got him elected mayor in 1954. At once he embarked on a series of major projects to rehabilitate the city. First he built the Metro. Inaugurated in 1966, it soon established itself as one of the world's great underground traffic systems; its rubber-wheeled trains serve 58 beautifully decorated stations, six of them linked to underground complexes that provide weatherproof access to hotels, office buildings, banks, and shops. Then, in the year of Canada's centennial, Drapeau presided over a great world fair—EXPO 67—that attracted 50 million visitors. Nearly as many came to the Montreal Olympics, held nine years later; but by that time, the great run of success was ending. Canada failed to win any gold medals, and the cost nearly bankrupted the city, which had already been hit by an economic downturn.

Slow growth in the 1970s, combined with the decision of many large firms to move their headquarters to Toronto, caused Montreal to lose its position as the country's leading manufacturing center—but only by a small margin. It remains one of the world's greatest inland ports, as well as the hub of Canada's transcontinental communications network. Canadian National and Canadian Pacific have their company headquarters here, as do such other firms as Air Canada, the International Civil Aviation Organization, and the International Air Transport Association. Appropriately enough for a city that has been dubbed the "Paris of North America," Montreal is an international center of fashion.

Quebec City lies almost 170 miles downstream, on a high promontory above the St. Lawrence at a point where the river narrows to a width of little more than 3,000 feet. Between the two cities, the old riverside roads have the look of extended villages, with a more or less continuous line of houses that thickens every few miles around a church, a few bigger residences, and a street of shops. The houses themselves, with their gracefully sloping roofs, small windows, and low doorways, which open directly on the street, are reminiscent of Brittany. Behind them, long narrow fields are aligned so that each farm has a river frontage.

This distinctive pattern is a legacy of the early French colonists' seigneurial system, an institutional form of land distribution practiced until 1854, by which the land was let in lots to tenant farmers by a small propertied class. Although inspired by an archaic feudalism, the riparian settlements offered many advantages, including easy access to the rivers, which were the main thoroughfares, and the encouragement of useful community initiatives and of general sociability.

A sense of antiquity pervades Quebec City itself. It is, after all, the oldest North American city and the only one with a city wall, which encloses a citadel, cobbled streets, and the greatest concentration of 17th- and 18th-century buildings in North America. Its old-world atmosphere has always made it attractive to European visitors; the 19th-century English poet Matthew Arnold considered it "the most interesting thing by much that I have seen on this continent." Charles Dickens noted, "It is a place not to be forgotten or mixed up in the mind with other places, or altered for a moment in the crowd of scenes a traveler can recall."

For more than two centuries after it was founded in 1608, Quebec City was Canada's major port, as well as a political and military capital. But the long delay in establishing a rail link to the city, and the improvements that enabled oceangoing vessels to sail directly to Montreal, reduced Quebec City's economic importance in the mid-19th century, leaving it a provincial administrative center.

In the mid-1980s, the service industries employed 4 out of 5 of the city's workers. Most of the others worked in industries—such as newsprint fabrication and grain milling—that depend for their raw materials on the port, which is still crucial to Quebec life. Another substantial group are civil servants, many of them employed in the Upper Town's National Assembly, an imposing French Renaissance-inspired building outside the city wall in an area of luxurious high-rise hotels, conven-tion centers, a busy underground shopping complex, and the other trappings of a modern provincial capital.

Below Quebec City, the St. Lawrence River steadily widens, making navigation relatively easy for the 12,000 ships that use it each year. From December to April, even the saltwater sections of the seaway freeze over. But the river is so important to Canada's trade that it is kept permanently open by about a dozen of Canada's 22 icebreakers, which

1

together represent more than 20 percent of the world's total. Beyond the Gaspé Peninsula, where seals bask and tourists gather to watch migrating whales, the river empties into the broad Gulf of St. Lawrence, open here to the four Maritime Provinces.

The Maritimes are a world apart. Historically, the provinces have earned their living from the sea. They were the first Canadian territories to be settled, and the transatlantic connection is maintained in the primarily British bloodlines of the people. Relatively untouched by the postwar waves of immigration, the Maritimers take pride in their distinctness, looking amicably toward New England to the south but regarding most of North America with suspicion tinged with envy. For decades, their region has been one of the poorest in Canada; recent offshore oil

and natural-gas discoveries have offered hope of regeneration.

Each province has a personality of its own. Tucked under the Gaspé Peninsula between Quebec and Maine, New Brunswick is a land of wood and water. Atlantic breakers crash along its extensive shoreline, which experiences the highest tides in the world—as high as 48.5 feet—in the Bay of Fundy. Inland, its rolling hills are covered with deciduous forests that burn brilliant red in the autumn. Many of the trees are sugar maples, whose sweet sap is an important local resource and whose leaf has, since 1965, adorned the national flag of Canada.

The mellow New Brunswick landscapes and small-scale society—its provincial capital, Fredericton, has a population of fewer than 50,000—belie the province's troubled past. With neighboring Nova Scotia, New Brunswick

originally formed the French province of Acadia. In 1713, the French ceded Acadia to the British under the terms of the Treaty of Utrecht. Four decades later, when tensions were high between Britain and France, the British responded to their Acadian subjects' uncertain loyalties by deporting three quarters of the population. Some returned—about one third of the present population being French-speakers—but they were destined to remain a minority after the American War of Independence, when New Brunswick was separated from Nova Scotia to give living space to many of the Loyalists who had left the fledgling United States.

Prince Edward Island, an hour's ferry ride from New Brunswick across the Northumberland Strait, is Canada's smallest province—less than one two-hundredth the size of Quebec and less than one thousandth of the Canadian landmass as a whole. Known to its earliest inhabitants, the Micmac Indians, as Abegweit, "the cradle in the waves," the province has also been described, less eloquently, as "Spud Island"—a reference to the potatoes that, nourished by the island's fertile red soil, used to dominate the province's economy. The provincial emblem of three small oak trees beneath a larger oak and its motto, The small under the protection of the great, were originally chosen to reflect the province's dependency on Britain; but they also aptly describe the province's current position in the Canadian federation.

Jutting into the North Atlantic like a giant lobster, Nova Scotia is tenuously linked to the mainland by a narrow isthmus at the top of the Bay of Fundy. As its name implies, the province has a strong Scottish connection; in Canada as a whole, more than 10 percent of the

In Quebec's Gaspé Peninsula, a craftsman locally renowned for his distinctive maplewood carvings of people and animals poses with three painted masks. A tradition of folk sculpture has developed among woodworkers in the area with time on their hands in the winter months.

28

population is of Scottish origin, but in Nova Scotia the proportion rises to about 50 percent. On Cape Breton Island, the northern extremity of the province, Gaelic is still spoken by some of the inhabitants. In places the land, too, with its rocky shoreline, boggy uplands, and acid-soiled heaths, is reminiscent of the Scottish Highlands.

But Nova Scotia is actually a mosaic of contrasting landscapes and half a dozen cultural influences. These include contributions from the French, who tried to control the region by building a mighty fort at Louisburg on Cape Breton Island. Irish refugees escaping the potato famines of the 1840s settled here. So did Germans, who es-

tablished the province's largest fishing port at Lunenburg, whose shipyards constructed the famous racing schooner *Bluenose*—a once-common sobriquet bestowed on the natives of the province as a whole.

A maritime economy has always been important to Nova Scotia. Its capital, Halifax, the largest city on Canada's eastern seaboard, was established in 1749 as an English fortress. Its southerly location facing the open ocean, which ensures that its port rarely ices up in winter, encouraged its growth. By the following century, Halifax had become the main gateway for Canada's exports. The great Cunard Company was founded here, and in World War I

and World War II, the city served as a vital staging area for North Atlantic convoys. Although its prosperity has diminished since World War II, offshore oil discoveries in the early 1980s hold out hope of renewed growth.

Newfoundland's fortunes have been linked to the sea since 1497, when the island after which the province is named was discovered by John Cabot, a Genoese navigator in the service of the English king. Cabot was searching for the Northwest Passage, the legendary sea route to the Orient, but found instead the teeming fishing grounds of the Grand Banks, a portion of Canada's continental shelf southwest of Cabot's Terra Nova. Fishermen from the

1

Wood houses nestling on the rugged north side of St. John's Harbor in Newfoundland face a channel giving access to the Atlantic Ocean. This inlet near the fishing grounds of Grand Banks has been a base for fishermen since its discovery by Genoese navigator John Cabot in 1497.

Basque region, Portugal, and France followed in Cabot's wake, but it was the British who first colonized Newfoundland's rocky, indented coastline. With 92 percent of Newfoundland's population of 563,000 claiming to be descended from West Country English or southern Irish settlers, the province still echoes its transatlantic inheritance—literally so, for the inhabitants have taken the Irish brogue and the West Country dialect and turned them together into one of Canada's most distinctive accents.

Nearly a quarter of the population lives in St. John's—named, according to folklore, after the feast day on which Cabot dropped anchor in the harbor. It is a perfect anchorage, sheltered from the open sea by a narrow channel and protected from gales by the high hills on which the present city stands. Since the center was ravaged five times by fire in the 19th century, none of the original colonial buildings survive, but the salty flavor of North America's oldest fishing port lingers along the waterfront, with its characteristic backdrop of tightly packed, flat-roofed houses of painted wood.

In the rest of Newfoundland, the settlements are scattered and remote, some consisting of just a few wooden houses that can be reached only by boat. Life in these communities has always been difficult. Rocky soil and a harsh climate make barely 1 acre in 1,000 fit for farming, and the traditional activities of fishing and sealing are fraught with their own peculiar dangers. Icebergs, concealed by the fogs that shroud the Grand Banks for 120 days each year, are a persistent menace; the *Titanic* went down 92.5 miles to the south in 1912. The victims among the local fishing community can be reckoned in terms of hundreds of vessels and thousands of lives.

Since the end of World War I, even the hard-earned harvest of the waters has not been capable of sustaining the provincial economy. During the Great Depression, Newfoundland in fact did become bankrupt. Though generously endowed with minerals and timber, the province has, even in the 1980s, an earned income level that is half the national average and an unemployment rate that may reach 50 percent in winter. Like Nova Scotia, Newfoundland pins its hopes for a brighter economic future on a potential oil and gas bonanza; the Hibernia field 188 miles offshore contains an estimated one billion barrels of crude oil.

A 19-mile strait separates the Island of Newfoundland, home to 80 percent of the province's population, from its mainland dependency of Labrador, but that narrow gap also separates the maritime world of the Atlantic Provinces from the great granite plateau known as the Canadian Shield. The Shield was formed more than 600 million years ago; but within the last 20,000 years, it has been extensively changed by ice sheets. During their advance, the ice sheets scooped out depressions that, as the ice retreated, filled with fresh water. These are the Canadian Lakes, which include giants such as the Great Bear and Great Slave, and thousands of smaller bodies of water that would be considered large by European standards, but in Canada are barely noticed except by cartographers. The retreating ice sheets further shaped the Newfoundland landscape by depositing in their wake huge amounts of glacial debris. The litter choked the Shield's drainage systems,

1

creating vast tracts of peaty bog called muskeg, which now cover about 400,000 square miles of territory. Where the ice had not actually scoured the land right down to bedrock, vegetation established itself—forests of spruce, pine, and fir as far northeast as Churchill, on Hudson Bay, and a great sweep of arctic tundra beyond.

A terrible winter climate, voracious black flies, appalling communications, and the sheer loneliness of it have made the Shield a barrier to mass settlement—yet this is Canada's main treasure trove of resources. The few communities that have been established are mostly one-industry towns, many of them accessible only to aircraft equipped with floats or skis. When the resources that created them, be they timber, minerals, or water power, run out, the inhabitants generally depart for more prosperous climes, leaving a scattering of ghost towns to increase the prevailing mood of abandonment.

Yet other developments thrive. The largest and most controversial is the James Bay project, a monumental hydroelectric undertaking in northern Quebec. Costing $15 billion (Canadian), the station has five dams, the largest of which is 525 feet high, as well as a tiered spillway three times the height of Niagara Falls, feeding the world's largest underground powerhouse. But the project has attracted much criticism—not only on grounds of cost, but also for its effect on local native peoples and the environment. Whole villages have been uprooted and vast areas of wilderness have been inundated by artificial lakes.

The non-native inhabitants of James Bay and other scattered Canadian Shield settlements try to reproduce life in the south as far as the climate allows.

EARNING A LIVING FROM SHELLFISH

A lobster painted on an outbuilding advertises the product of a processing factory in Caraquet, New Brunswick.

Tucked between Maine and the Gulf of St. Lawrence, New Brunswick has always had close links with the sea. But few of its towns depend as heavily for their livelihood on the sea as Caraquet on Chaleur Bay, center of a thriving seafood industry.

Each year, boats working out of the port of Caraquet haul in 19,000 long tons of crab and lobster from traps set in the waters of the bay. Two processing plants employ hundreds of townspeople to steam, shuck, and clean the catch before packaging it for distribution to all parts of Canada and the United States.

But the wilderness is always close, pressing in on them and confining them for months on end to their centrally heated prefabricated cubes. In Churchill, for example, people venture out only with caution during the autumn, when the area receives a large influx of polar bears that have even taken to pillaging the town dump.

The western edge of the Shield is reached in southeastern Manitoba. Its moss-draped spruces and beaver ponds give way to scrubby copses and then to flat grasslands that stretch across the southern part of the Prairie Provinces until, 715 miles to the west, they rise into the Rockies. Viewed from the Canadian Pacific Railway (CPR) or from the Trans-Canada Highway, the 4,888-mile east-west road link that was completed in 1970, the landscape soon palls. The terrain's monotonous lack of

relief is intensified by the regimented spacing of the settlements; the gridlike layout of the roads; the checkerboard pattern of the wheat fields; and predictable as milestones, the towering bulk of grain elevators, or warehouses in which cereals are hoisted aloft for storage so that gravity can help in the loading of transshipment vehicles.

The land is not entirely flat and treeless, however. In the Cypress Hills of Saskatchewan, the prairie rises into a rolling, forested upland that offers sanctuary to deer, moose, and beaver, while everywhere shallow hollows and sloughs shelter stands of poplar and provide breeding grounds for half of North America's wildfowl.

There are also contrasts between the people and life-styles of the Prairie Provinces. The first European settlers were British and French fur trappers, who intermarried with the indigenous

Fishing boats lie at anchor in the town's harbor.

At the Chaleur Bay packing plant, workers extract meat from crab legs.

Indians. (Their descendants, called the Métis, still constitute approximately 1 percent of the population.) Large-scale colonization did not really get under way, however, until the close of the 19th century, when the Canadian Pacific Railway made the west accessible to poor immigrants from all over Europe. Many of them transplanted their native cultures to the acres of land that they were allotted. Scattered throughout the region, the bulbous spires of Russian Orthodox churches mark the locations of Ukrainian communities. Every August, the world's largest Icelandic settlement outside the home country celebrates its heritage with a three-day-long festival in Gimli, Manitoba. And in Saskatchewan, the Doukhobors, a sect of Russian religious dissenters who escaped persecution in the Caucasus with the help of Leo Tolstoy and English Quakers, hold the *sobranyas* that serve as both religious services and community meetings.

Wheat and barley are the traditional mainstays of the Prairies; but, although the provinces are still responsible for producing nearly 40 million tons of grain each year, their economies have diverged since World War II. The changes are reflected in the character of the major urban centers. Winnipeg, provincial capital of Manitoba and the country's fifth-largest city with almost 600,000 inhabitants, is the region's financial center. From a collection of shacks at the time of its incorporation in 1873, Winnipeg has developed into a sophisticated urban community, boasting its own opera company, internationally acclaimed ballet troupe, and symphony orchestra. Regina, the capital of the grain-growing province of Saskatchewan, is set in an unrelieved prairie. It has come a long way since its origins as a railroad siding nicknamed Pile o' Bones because its first industry was transporting to eastern glue factories the buffalo carcasses left by hunters to bleach on the prairies.

In Alberta, the wheat fields give way to cattle ranches and oil fields, which at the time of the oil boom made the province the richest in Canada. Edmonton, the provincial capital and also North America's northernmost big city, was originally a fur-trading outpost. It is now a major petrochemical center. Edmonton is also the largest Canadian city in terms of area, the most rapidly growing in recent decades, and the most unfinished: It has been continuously redeveloped since the 1950s, with ever more glass and steel. Among other signs of new wealth, Edmonton had in the mid-1980s the world's largest shopping mall, eight city blocks long and three blocks wide.

1

Calgary, Alberta's other large town, also looks as though it has just been uncrated. Nicknamed Cowtown because of its ranching associations, it is today the headquarters of the national oil and gas industries that supply half of Canada's needs; but it recalls its bovine heritage each summer, when thousands of would-be cowhands and tourists descend there for the rodeo known as the Calgary Stampede.

From the most uniform of Canada's regions, the Canadian Pacific Railway snakes west to the most diverse, climbing to 5,330 feet at Kicking Horse Pass in the Rocky Mountains. This is the Western Cordillera. Beyond, the railroad snakes down the other side of the Great Divide into British Columbia, Canada's window on the Pacific. It is a region of superlatives, with Canada's wettest and mildest climate, highest mountains, and densest forests containing the tallest and thickest trees. In the varied habitats of its three main subregions—the monumental fir and cedar forests of the Pacific Coast, the sagebrush and cactus belt of the dry interior plateau, and the alpine pastures of the Rockies—there are more species of plants and animals than are found anywhere else in the country. Canadian humorist Stephen Leacock thought it an equally benign habitat for people: He described it as "an ideal home for the human race, not too cold, not too hot, not too wet, not too dry, except in the hotels, a thing which time may remedy." (It has.)

In resources, too, British Columbia is blessed with variety. Although it has only about 15 percent of Canada's total area of forests, it produces two thirds of the country's sawed lumber, most of its plywood, and a quarter of its chemical

A steer and its teenage rider part company during the Little Britches Rodeo in High River, Alberta. At this event, the largest children's rodeo in western Canada, boys and girls seven years and older show their mettle in events such as calf roping, steer wrestling, and bronco busting.

pulp. With a smaller proportion of cultivated land than any province except Newfoundland, it is nonetheless responsible for 5 percent of Canada's agricultural output, aided by the longest growing season in the country. Offshore, no fewer than 300 species of fish are found, sustaining a commercial fishery worth $361 million (Canadian) in 1983. Various mining operations—mainly coal and copper—employ about 5 percent of the work force, and there

is hydroelectric power, petroleum, and natural gas to spare.

Among the Indians who settled British Columbia's coast 6,000 to 8,000 years ago, the abundance of resources encouraged the development of North America's most elaborate native culture. Their rich heritage was typified by the carving of totem poles and by the legendary potlatch ceremony, in which opulent hoards of food and artifacts were bestowed on neighboring tribes in

the most extravagant displays of conspicuous generosity.

The first European settlements were founded by fur traders in the early 19th century. There were fewer than 1,000 colonists by 1850, but the discovery of gold on the Fraser River in 1858 increased the population thirtyfold within the year. The vast majority of the newcomers were of British origin; in the late 19th century, the only other settlers who came in notable numbers

The glittering lights of Vancouver,
reflected green on passing clouds,
spread southward away from the
harbor frontage on Burrard Inlet. The
city is Canada's main Pacific port;
with more than one million citizens,
Vancouver is home to half the population of British Columbia.

were the Chinese. They were brought in as laborers to build the CPR, whose construction had been a condition of the colony's entry to the confederation. Since then, the British element has been diluted by newcomers from other parts of Europe, from Vietnam, and Japan, as well as by Canadians from other provinces, attracted across the Great Divide by the high standard of living, unrivaled recreational facilities, and the relaxed life-style offered by Canada's own, cooler California.

Studiedly British manners set the tone in Victoria, the capital of the province. The city stands on the southern tip of Vancouver Island, which dips below the 49th parallel to within 80 miles of Seattle. Afternoon tea is still served at the Empress Hotel in Victoria, roses bloom in some of the best-kept gardens in Canada, and in a nearby suburb is a re-creation of a Shakespearean-era village that includes a thatch-roofed replica of Anne Hathaway's cottage. The city is a favorite destination for retired people, and it has the highest proportion of residents aged 65 and older in all of Canada.

Vancouver itself, the largest city in British Columbia and the third largest in Canada, with 1.3 million people in its metropolitan area, lies across the Strait of Georgia, in the southwest corner of the Canadian mainland. Surrounded on three sides by water, with wooded mountains reaching almost to the shoreline and, beyond them, distant snowy peaks, it has one of the most splendid settings any urban center could hope for. These natural advantages must have dulled the critical senses of its original planners, because the early settlement that grew from its Gastown waterfront was laid out on a grid pattern that made few concessions

to natural features. At the same time, the strong desire for home ownership led to an undisciplined sprawl of suburbs climbing over the surrounding hills. Vancouver still has more privately owned single family homes than either Toronto or Montreal—in fact, well over twice as many as the latter. Since the 1960s, however, the downtown area has been rehabilitated with high-rise buildings, their proportions kept in scale by the mountain backdrop. And the numerous large city parks, the benign presence of water, and the easy access to unspoiled country all contribute to an urban environment envied by many North Americans on both sides of the border.

Despite British Columbia's abundant and widespread resources, no other province has such a high concentration of population in such a relatively small area. Two thirds of British Columbians live in the southwest. North of Prince Rupert, halfway up the province, the largest town has a population of fewer than 15,000. Across the southern boundary of the Yukon Territory, the population density diminishes even more, with roughly one grizzly bear to every four people. "If you are confronted by a bear," one tourist guide to the Yukon advises, "the best policy is simply to back away slowly and quietly. Do not run, yell, or scream. Remember that the wilderness of the Yukon is nothing to be afraid of." According to *The Canadian Encyclopedia*, about one visitor in two million to the national parks pays no attention to this advice, with sometimes fatal results.

Exposed to snow for up to nine months each year, the Yukon's towering mountains and forested valleys are virtually unpeopled but, by the same token, virtually unspoiled. Its repose

1

The 480-mile-long Dempster Highway slices northward through both forest land and tundra in the Yukon Territory. Running from Dawson to Inuvik in the Northwest Territories, the highway is the most northerly to be found in the Americas.

has been shattered only once, in the brief fin-de-siècle frenzy of the Klondike Gold Rush. Almost overnight, Dawson, the capital, was transformed from an Indian salmon-drying station into a boomtown of 16,000 adventurers, whose spiritual and bodily needs were catered to by seven clergymen, eight members of the Salvation Army, and a cadre of Belgian prostitutes. By the end of the century, the boom was over; and by 1981, the town's population had dwindled to 697—twenty-eight years after its demise was formally announced by the transfer of the capital to Whitehorse.

Like its predecessor's, Whitehorse's prosperity had its roots in the Yukon Territory's mineral wealth, this time in the form of silver, copper, and lead-zinc, which attracted a growing, if ever changing, population in the 1960s and 1970s. But the difficulties and expense

concomitant with exploiting and transporting goods in such rugged terrain make the territory particularly vulnerable to fluctuations in world markets. In 1982, for example, the Cyprus-Anvil lead-zinc mining concern, which accounted for approximately 40 percent of the value of the territorial product, shut its doors and pushed unemployment in the territory above 15 percent.

To the east of the Mackenzie River, the longest in Canada, the population is even more dispersed, with just one person to every 30 square miles. This region is known as the Barren Lands of the Northwest Territories, and it occupies more than one third of the Canadian landmass. The area's 43,000 inhabitants are scattered throughout 64 small communities, of which the largest is the capital, Yellowknife—and even the citizens who live here in the capital city number no more than 9,500.

More than half the territories' inhabitants are either native Indians or Eskimo—now always known in Canada by their chosen name, Inuit. For both peoples, trapping, hunting, and fishing have retained much traditional importance; but today these peoples live mainly in modern settlements with access to health services, schools, and unemployment benefits. The rest of the population are mostly short-term contract workers employed in services and in mining, by far the most important economic base for the region. Like the James Bay project, many of the industrial developments made here have gone ahead in spite of opposition from the indigenous peoples and in defiance of their claims to traditional lands, which, since the expansion of native-rights organizations in the 1970s, have made the Far North something of a political battleground.

Although in human terms they are the loneliest part of the "Great Lone Land," the Northwest Territories are crowded with wildlife during the few brief weeks of summer, when snow melts to reveal a landscape patterned with polygonal cracks and strange domes created by the action of ice in the still-frozen ground. Insects swarm over ponds crawling with larvae, providing food for the millions of waders and wildfowl that return each year to breed on the Barrens. Thousands of caribou file across the tundra, growing fat on lichens, sedges, and grasses and sometimes drowning by the hundreds as they attempt to cross rivers swollen by meltwater. By September, the birds have flown south and the caribou have turned their noses toward the treeline, trailed by wolves. One month later, the only large animals left are musk oxen, arctic foxes, and polar bears, along with

Smiling brothers play on a sled in Grise Fjord, Canada's northernmost Inuit settlement. Located 625 miles above the Arctic Circle on the south coast of Ellesmere Island, the town was established by the government in 1953 to provide improved services for the native population.

ptarmigan, ravens, and gyrfalcons; and for the next eight months, a vast silence pervades the land.

The American writer Jack London, who participated in the 1897-1898 Klondike Gold Rush, later described the bitter landscape of the Far North in winter, when the temperature sometimes remains below a bone-chilling −4° F. for more than four months at a time. "The land itself was a desolation, lifeless, without movement, so lone and cold that the spirit of it was not even that of sadness. There was a hint in it of laughter, but of a laughter more terrible than any sadness—a laughter that was mirthless as the smile of the Sphinx, a laughter cold as the frost and partaking of the grimness of infallibility. It was the masterful and incommunicable wisdom of eternity laughing at the futility of life and the effort of life."

Most Canadians have no firsthand experience of the Far North, although every winter they are reminded of its presence when arctic winds sweep down on the populous belt below, threatening the life of the farmer caught in a blizzard between barn and house, severely disrupting life in the cities, and pushing energy consumption to the highest level in the world. But in a country that has developed the concept of "nordicity" to explain its special identity, the Far North is as much a state of consciousness as a physical reality. Heir to two mutually antagonistic cultures and overshadowed by a third, Canada has been defined as a nation not so much by history as by its immense, forbidding, and unconquerable geography.

The Canadian writer Michael Ignatieff makes the point well. "It is hard to love a country if it doesn't also awaken a measure of awe and fear. Soviet exiles love Russia because and not in spite of the fact that it devours so many of its finest citizens. Americans love America because, in part, they also fear it. In Europe, the sources of fear are historical: History with a capital *H* rifling the writing desk, smashing up the cabinets, yanking the children out of bed. In Canada, history happens somewhere else. Most of us went there in the first place to get out of history's way. We do not fear our history as the Russians do, or love it as the Americans do. But we found our own fear: the scrabbling of the black bear's claws at the screen door, the creaking silence of the woods, the cold." ☐

THE LOOK OF THE LAND

Canada is a country of boundless space and noble vistas. Even the comparatively populous belt just north of the border with the United States boasts scenery as wild as any in the world; and a traveler on the nation's main artery, the Trans-Canada Highway, passes through a succession of memorable landscapes.

The route starts in the Maritime Provinces, where ancient rocks front the Atlantic with cliffs as gray as the sea. Farther west, in Quebec, short excursions from the highway take the voyager to the Gulf of St. Lawrence and to the woods and waters of the Canadian Shield. In neighboring Ontario, the route skirts the Great Lakes, passing through farmland and a labyrinth of wooded lakes and rivers. Starting just over the Manitoba border, the flatlands of the Prairie Provinces stretch across more than 800 miles of rich agricultural land to the foothills of the Rockies. Beyond that great barrier, the way descends to Canada's other ocean, on British Columbia's Pacific shore.

Farming and fishing coexist on Prince Edward Island.

Trees cap a dramatic stack in New Brunswick.

A lighthouse marks Newfoundland's easterly point.

Wooded hills loom behind New Brunswick crofts.

Canada's eastern fringe, the chilly waters of the Atlantic lap the coastline of Cape Breton Island, part of the province of Nova Scotia.

41

A bridge spans a river near Causapscal in Quebec.

Forest yields to pasture near the St. Lawrence estuary.

Dusk falls on a lake in the Laurentian Mountains.

Gigantic Percé Rock tips Quebec's Gaspé Peninsula.

Reflected in the glassy waters of the St. Maurice River near Shawinigan in Quebec, autumn foliage glows in the primeval forests that stretch

unbroken for hundreds of miles northward into the province's virtually unpopulated wilderness.

The Aguasabon River surges through a cleft it has cut on its way to swell the waters of Lake Superior near the town of Terrace Bay in Ontario.

Checkerboard fields fill Ontario's Bruce Peninsula.

Silos and a barn rise by a meadow near Ottawa.

Pale birches ring Old Woman Bay on Lake Superior.

A homestead glows amid forest near English River.

Mechanical harvesters reap grain west of Regina.

Maple Creek, Saskatchewan, basks in the prairie sun.

Buffalo feed in Manitoba's Riding Mountain Park.

Erosion scars Alberta's fossil-rich Dinosaur Park,

A full moon glimmers in the waning of a summer evening above Regina, capital of Saskatchewan. The grain fields, which cover 30 percent of the

...ovince, sweep right up to the outskirts of its chief town.

47

Log cabins at Gang Ranch recall the Alps.

A rancher's herd crosses a plateau.

West of Calgary, hills spread behind an early church.

Driftwood punctuates the sands of Vancouver Island.

Near Alberta's western boundary, where the Rockies break the monotony of the prairies, low clouds wreath the crags of the Canadian cordillera.

The ranges and plateaux of the mountain belt stretch almost 440 miles westward across British Columbia to end in the fjords of the Pacific Coast.

In a 19th-century drawing, a heavily clad trapper and his wife trudge through a winter landscape with their bag of game birds. The couple's snowshoes and sledge are among the many accoutrements the early settlers borrowed from native Indian life.

TWIN PILLARS OF A NATION

Imagine a Victorian traveler in time from the Canada of the 1860s waking up in the Canada of the 1980s. Everything would astonish him: the 24 lanes of superhighway north of Toronto where once there was a dusty track; the featureless miles of suburban homes where before there stood lonely stone farmhouses surrounded by the bush; the light, casual dress of the passersby instead of collars, crinolines, and fustian; the height and obvious good health of Canadians in the 1980s in place of barefoot ragamuffins and bent, prematurely wizened men aged by labor in the fields. There would be much for the time traveler to envy in the speed, convenience, and vitality of the new Canada; much to fear in the pace and noise of the huge cities; and maybe something to regret in the passing of the original peaceful rural order. But perhaps what would surprise the Victorian time traveler more than anything else is that Canada should still exist at all.

In 1867, when Canada became a nation, it was, as it still is in the 1980s, a country composed of regions confronted by a far more powerful and self-assertive neighbor along nearly 5,000 miles of shared border. Then as now, Canada was divided rather than united by geography, religion, and language. Yet somehow, against all the odds of its own divisions, the nation has in the intervening years not merely survived but prospered, to grow into a land that

ranks among the top 10 industrialized economies in the world.

Although the nation is little more than a century old, the lands it occupies are ages older, and the history of human settlement within their borders has its origins in the furthest mists of time. No one is sure when the first people arrived, but it was probably some 30,000 years ago; the earliest artifact found in Canada, a caribou bone notched for use as a scraper, has been carbon-dated to 25,000 B.C.

What is generally agreed is that the original settlers were hunter-gatherers from the Asian mainland who made their way over a land bridge crossing what is now the Bering Strait. The bridge owed its existence to Ice Age glaciation, which had locked up so much water that sea level dropped by perhaps 400 feet. But the glaciers also made a great part of Canada uninhabitable. Only a narrow corridor, in places no more than 25 miles wide, lay open through the Mackenzie River valley to the east of the Rockies, drawing hunters southward into the unpeopled continent that stretched before them. Around 18,000 B.C., when the Ice Age was at its peak, even that access closed up. The tribes that had once hunted in the valley were forced to take refuge on the ice-free plains of Alaska or in the warmer lands to the south.

But then the ice, in its great and ponderous cycle, again receded: From approximately 13,000 B.C., a further

2

wave of Asian migrants made the trek east. Drawn on by good hunting and pressed by newcomers at their heels, the migrants eventually populated the entire American continent, from the retreating northern ice to its southern, near-Antarctic tip.

Those who remained in the sub-Arctic forests that extended from the ice to the Great Lakes and the plains beyond developed their own rich, tribal culture, as well as a life-style that provided a reasonably comfortable existence despite the long, harsh winters

and the minimal agriculture they practiced. Farther north, in the true Arctic, lived a few thousand Inuit—Eskimo, as the forest dwellers called them—a people ethnically distinct and the last of the migrants from Asia.

However, by the present millennium, the natives no longer had the land to themselves. This time the newcomers came by sea, across the wide North Atlantic; and although their numbers were few, they were shortly to change the continent beyond recognition.

The first visitors to leave traces of

their presence were Vikings, sailing from bases they had established in Iceland and Greenland. Their bards told the story of the voyage in the *Vinland Saga,* an epic, written much later, that described how one Leif Ericsson inspected the coasts of "Markland" and "Vinland"—probably Nova Scotia and Newfoundland—in about 1000 A.D., organizing a settlement in Vinland the following year. But the accounts are geographically vague and might not have been taken for historical fact were it not for the discovery of archaeolog-

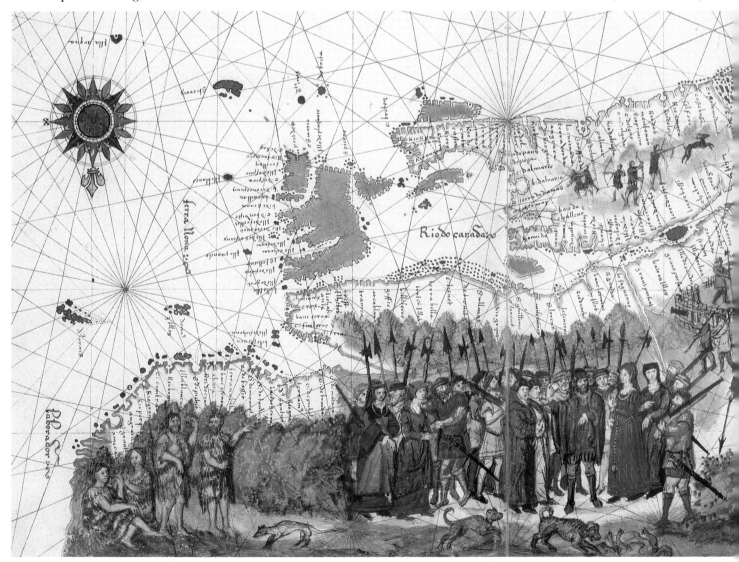

ical evidence to support them. The remains of a Scandinavian-style village were discovered in 1964 at L'Anse aux Meadows on Newfoundland's northern tip, complete with a smithy for forging iron—a technique unknown to the native peoples. But Viking settlement, such as it was, was marginal and seems to have endured the combination of hard winters and native hostility for only a few years.

Canada next enters recorded history almost five centuries later in 1497, with the voyage of John Cabot. In the wake

One of the earliest maps of the North American coast depicts the 1542 expedition led by the Sieur de Roberval to set up France's first colony in Canada. Plagued by illness and internal dissension, the settlement near Quebec lasted less than a year.

of Columbus's voyage to the New World, King Henry VII of England granted Cabot letters patent to travel across the Atlantic to "seek out, discover, and find whatsoever isles, countries, regions, or provinces of the heathen and infidels wheresoever they be, which before this time have been unknown to all Christians." The land that he discovered—the Newfoundland coastline—appeared chill and worthless, but Cabot took possession of it in the name of his royal master.

Perhaps more important, he found fish—cod in such quantity that, the chroniclers recorded, they "sometimes stayed his shippes." Word of these wondrous shoals spread quickly, and soon Europe's hardiest fishermen—from England, from Portugal, and increasingly from France—were regularly trawling the Grand Banks. But beyond a few huts for shelter while they dried and salted their catch, they never established a settlement.

Nonetheless, these early incursions pointed the way to the route that was to open the interior of the country. This course led through the Gulf of St. Lawrence and up the St. Lawrence River, the waterway around which the future nation was to be built. Two great names above all others are associated with the exploration of the St. Lawrence, and both of them are French.

The first is that of a tough Breton sailor who was convinced that the river might provide the legendary northwest passage to the untold wealth of the Orient. Between 1534 and 1543, Jacques Cartier made three expeditions to the area; on the second trip he traveled about 700 miles upstream until rapids barred the way. He christened the hill at which his passage was halted Mont Réal—a name adopted for the city that

subsequently sprouted at its base. The troublesome cataracts themselves were later given the name Lachine—China—in honor of the land of riches that was believed to be waiting beyond them. On his third and final voyage, Cartier brought settlers with him, but the colony he tried to establish was a short-lived failure. The domain of the optimistically named New France was soon abandoned to its original owners, the Indians.

The dream of New France was nonetheless to be realized early in the following century by the other French founding father, Samuel de Champlain. What attracted Champlain to Canada was a new trade that was to become the lifeblood of the growing nation and one that had its roots in European fashion. In the latter part of the 16th century, a penchant for wide-brimmed felt hats spread, and it was soon discovered that no material was more suitable for making them than the soft and easily matted underfur of the Canadian beaver. Trade in the pelts—previously merely a sideline practiced by some of the St. Lawrence fishermen in their dealings with the coastal Indians—suddenly grew into a big business.

Champlain first visited the St. Lawrence in 1603. He returned the next year in company with an enterprising aristocrat, the Sieur de Monts, to set up a trading colony in the Bay of Fundy. But the interior beckoned, and four years later, Champlain followed Cartier's old route up the St. Lawrence to build a wooden fort and trading post on a riverside hill the Indians called Quebec. This time, due in large part to the help of friendly Indians who taught the newcomers how to survive in the wilderness, the colony took hold.

2

For the remaining 27 years of his life, Champlain devoted himself to furthering Quebec's interests, despite lukewarm support from his patrons, who were more interested in turning a quick profit than in the lengthy business of colonization. In pursuit of his goal, Champlain explored the St. Lawrence River system as far as Lake Huron, built an economic base for settlement by successful fur trading, and propagandized tirelessly for the new colony back in France. His Indian alliances also drew him at one time into inconclusive war with the ferocious Iroquois, deadly enemies of the Huron and Algonquin Indians who had befriended him.

By the time Champlain died in 1635, the pattern of Canadian history for the next 130 years had been established. The principal players included the bold and resourceful *coureurs de bois,* canoe-borne adventurers who set out into the woods and along the countless tributaries of the St. Lawrence in search of furs to trap and friendly Indians to trade with. Then there was the hostile presence of unfriendly tribes, constantly on the lookout for unwary settlers. At one stage these tribes grew determined enough to launch an all-out assault on Montreal, which almost succeeded in taking the infant city by storm.

More threatening still for the French was the uneasy presence of another European power: To the south, the English were founding colonies that would one day become the United States of America. They had northern outposts, too: English settlements were established in Newfoundland in 1610 and in Nova Scotia in 1629. Later in the century, a source of continuing friction was created when a trading organization that brought the interests of the British directly into conflict with the

French trappers was established. This was the Hudson's Bay Company, to which the king of England, Charles II, in 1670 blithely granted monopoly trading rights over the whole catchment area surrounding the bay. This huge, unmapped domain was named Rupert's Land, in honor of the king's cousin who headed the list of investors.

Predictably, the outcome of the clash of interests was war. England and France were rivals in Europe, too; and when open conflict broke out there in 1689, the struggle quickly spread across the Atlantic. For almost three quarters of a century, North America was a battleground between the two settler communities. Even when peace was officially declared, as it was in 1697 and again in 1713, the resulting periods of calm were used only to rearm. Yet for all the murderous hostility of the local conflict, gains and losses in the struggle were determined more by the fate of armies in faraway Europe than in the colonies themselves. Thus, the British

won Acadia in 1713 as a reward for the Duke of Marlborough's victories in France, Germany, and Flanders during the War of the Spanish Succession.

The conclusion to this long period of struggle came with the French and Indian War, which broke out in 1754. This time, the start of hostilities in the colonies prefigured European conflict; indeed, the French and Indian War was one of the sparks that ignited the Seven Years' War in 1756. At first the French, though outnumbered, had the best of the fighting, and in 1756, when reinforcements arrived from France in the shape of 10,000 troops commanded by the brilliant Marquis Louis de Montcalm, they went on the offensive. But Britain responded by sending across the Atlantic a charismatic leader of its own, James Wolfe.

The decisive encounter between the two generals took place at Quebec in 1759. For nearly two months their armies confronted each other, feinting attacks and counterattacks in a deadly game of cat and mouse. Then, with winter drawing near, Wolfe decided that the time had come to cast his lot. He led his troops by boat to a daring night landing at a cove beneath the citadel, and his men ascended the supposedly insurmountable cliffs fronting the river. When day dawned, Montcalm awoke to find Wolfe's forces drawn up in line of battle on the Plains of Abraham, the plateau immediately outside the walls of his stronghold. In the ensuing battle, both commanders lost their lives; but the British emerged triumphant. Their victory proved a turning point in Canadian history. They followed up by capturing Montreal the next summer; and although the Seven Years' War dragged on in Europe until 1763, there were no compensating French victories to trade off against Britain's Canadian gains. The Peace of Paris confirmed the defeat: North America was to be British.

Yet if any British administrator of the day had felt inclined to be smug about this fact, the realities of the situation would quickly have disabused him. Though the rulers of French Canada returned to Europe after the Peace of Paris, taking much of the colony's homegrown middle class with them, the rest of the French-Canadian population of small farmers, traders, and trappers stayed in Canada. The British were confronted with ruling a community alien not only in religion—in 18th-century England, Catholics lacked many civil rights—but in political development as well.

The result was an uneasy cohabitation made possible only by considerable restraint on both sides. For their part, the French threw themselves back on their traditions—language, law, and the church—with a single objective in mind: *la survivance*, the survival of their way of life. Their English rulers were content not to challenge them. In 1774, the Quebec Act granted official recognition to French laws and customs and also acknowledged the special position held by the Catholic clergy, while in 1791 the French-speaking province got its own legislative assembly.

By then, a new factor had entered the balance. A rebellion in the British colonies to the south had developed into the American War of Independence. To the surprise of both sides in that struggle, the French population of Canada showed no inclination to make common cause against the colonial master. Survival, the French reasoned, would be easier as a French-speaking outpost of empire than as a tiny minority in an English-speaking continental republic. Even so, their position was not made easier by the arrival in their midst of thousands of Empire Loyalists fleeing the newly independent United States because they feared reprisals for their support of Britain.

The Constitutional Act of 1791 was framed partly to ease the resultant culture clash. By its terms, the old French inland colony of Canada was divided into two parts, Upper and Lower Canada, that corresponded with today's provinces of Ontario and Quebec. Lower Canada remained overwhelmingly French, but Upper Canada had an English-speaking majority; its own legislative assembly; and the language, laws, and religion the newly enlarged Anglophone community wanted.

The latter years of the 18th century saw another development crucial for the nation's future. The first steps were taken to open up the west. Progress came on two fronts, by land and by sea. Overland exploration had always been a by-product of the work of fur trappers as they sought fresh territories in which to hunt and trade. Competition intensified in 1775, when a band of Scottish merchants set up the North West Company in a direct challenge to the Hudson's Bay Company monopoly. In terms of discovery, the most spectacular results were the journeys of a young Northwester, Alexander Mackenzie, in search of a through route to the Pacific. On his first trip, he found the river that now bears his name and traced it, to his disappointment, to its mouth on the Arctic Ocean. Four years later, in 1793, he and nine others struggled by canoe and on foot from Fort Chipewyan in present-day Alberta across the Rockies; they reached the Pacific at the mouth of the Bella Coola River. Here, their paths touched those of the seaborne explorers: Captain James Cook, one of England's greatest mariners, had charted the future British Columbia coast while voyaging through the Bering Strait in 1778.

Fourteen years later, Captain George Vancouver of the British Navy, who

Champlain drew this plan of the Sainte Croix settlement, founded in 1604 on an island near the present U.S. border. Lack of wood and fresh water made it an unsuitable site; it was abandoned after a winter that cost the lives of 36 of the 80 settlers.

2

had been a midshipman on Cook's voyage, returned to explore the coast further and to make the first circumnavigation of the island that now bears his name. By 1800, the shape of the continent of North America was clearly known, although many of the details of its internal geography still remained to be filled in.

As the 19th century dawned, the constituent parts of the future federation of Canada were in place, but at that time their inhabitants had no thought of belonging to a united nation. They had only just attained their first measure of self-government, and their loyalties were first to Britain, then to their colony. Of the 10 provinces that make up the country today, the four western

ones were still wildernesses, while the loyal British colony of Newfoundland in the east was already cast in the independently minded mold that led it to reject union with the rest of the nation until after World War II.

Upper and Lower Canada formed the troubled core of the future confederation. In Lower Canada, the policy of survival was proving a success for the French community; far from fading away, as many observers expected, the population had multiplied, aided by some of the highest birthrates recorded anywhere in the world. By the 1820s, the great fur empire based in Montreal, once the center of French economic power, had collapsed, leaving the Hudson's Bay Company (which in 1821 had taken over the rival North West Com-

pany) in exclusive possession of the hinterland. Instead, the French settlers earned their living on the strip fields left over from the old French seigneurial system, in the fisheries of the St. Lawrence, and in the boatbuilding and timber yards.

But they did not have Lower Canada to themselves. The province had become a society divided against itself. The English-speaking minority, dour Scottish entrepreneurs such as businessmen James McGill and Simon McTavish, had first taken over the fur trade and, when that failed, had consolidated the British hold on banking, timber, shipping, and shipbuilding. (McGill also founded the celebrated university that bears his name.) The French-speakers resented the British

minority's domination of legal and eco-momic life; and in 1837, a rebellion was raised against it by the speaker of the province's legislative assembly, Louis Joseph Papineau. Although the revolt amounted to little more than some violent rioting that was easily put down by the military, it helped convince the authorities in London, who were still mindful of the British defeat in the American Revolution, that they must find a long-term solution to the problems of their divided colonies.

In Upper Canada, too, 1837 was a year of revolution. The vast majority of the population there was English speaking, but it was by no means of a single nationality. To its base population of Empire Loyalists and demobilized soldiers, the years after 1815 had added a steady stream of Scots and Ulster Irish, joined by hundreds of thousands of Irish Catholics fleeing starvation in their famine-stricken homeland. Yet Upper Canada's economic and political life continued to be dominated by a small and unrepresentative group, known to their enemies as the Family Compact, who were Tory in their politics and even more British than the British in their ideas and attitudes.

It was against this clique that the fighting newspaperman William Lyon Mackenzie raised the flag of revolt when word came through of Papineau's uprising in Montreal. Mackenzie managed to assemble a band of about 800 armed farmers and workers. But in the only major engagement of the rebellion, they were easily dispersed by a combined force of Regular soldiers and volunteers scared by Mackenzie's radicalism. In the wake of the troubles, British authorities sent an aristocratic envoy, Lord Durham, to seek out the causes of discontent. As a result of his

report, Upper and Lower Canada were reunited (primarily in order to appease the Anglophone community) and, in 1848, the joint colony was made self-governing in all matters except foreign affairs—rights subsequently extended to the Atlantic colonies also. These reforms did go some way to calm the unrest in the provinces. Even so, on the eve of confederation, the memory of the two revolts was still vivid enough to make it appear that Britain might lose her last foothold in North America if no long-term solution to the political weakness of the colonies were found.

In the end, the force that made Canada one nation came from south of the border. The people of the British colonies were witnesses as the United States plunged into the trauma of its civil war. Britain maintained its trading relations with the Confederacy, thereby infuriating the Union, which was busy creating one of the largest armies the world had ever seen. There were plenty of Yankee voices to be heard demanding a full-blown invasion of Canada in retaliation.

Against the American threat, there could be no real military defense, but there was the possibility of a moral one. A united, federal Dominion of Canada would surely give the most annexation-prone American pause—or so the British government hoped, when it added its considerable weight to the pro-

Federation movement that already existed in Canada itself. The result was the British North America Act of 1867, hurried through Parliament in London to create what the act solemnly declared to be "one Dominion under the name of Canada." The formula expressed a hope more than a reality, for only two out of the four Maritime colonies—New Brunswick and Nova Scotia—agreed at the time to accept confederation. (Prince Edward Island finally threw in its lot with the new nation six years later, while Newfoundland held out until 1949.)

But the stratagem worked. The United States respected the sovereignty of its new neighbor to the north, and under the leadership of its first prime minister, the Conservative Sir John A. Macdonald—one of the wiliest, most duplicitous, and hardest-drinking politicians ever to be the father of a country—Canada was at last a nation.

The first task that confronted the fledgling power was the taming of its own wild west. The territory was enormous. In 1869, Canada purchased the whole gigantic wilderness of Rupert's Land from the Hudson's Bay Company. Two years later, the young colony of British Columbia, inhabited largely by American miners drawn into Canada by the Fraser River gold rush, agreed to join the dominion on the promise of a transcontinental rail link; previously it communicated with the mother country by way of the 12,500-mile sea route around Cape Horn, bypassing Canada altogether. Macdonald himself was less than enthusiastic at the prospect of westward expansion. "I would be quite willing to leave that whole country a wilderness for the next half century," he declared. "But I fear

In a 19th-century colored lithograph, Plains Indians perform sympathetic magic by dancing dressed as the buffalo they intend to hunt. The Indians remained masters of Canada's prairies until the arrival of European settlers in the 19th century.

An 18th-century lithograph details the steps by which General Wolfe's British forces took Quebec in 1759. After a night landing at an almost unguarded path up the cliff protecting the city, the troops defeated the French the next day on the heights known as the Plains of Abraham.

that if Englishmen do not go there, Yankees will."

It was not a complete wilderness. The Hudson's Bay Company's old Red River post—more or less on the site of modern Winnipeg—had expanded into a thriving little settlement. In addition, a hardy population of 10,000 or so mixed-bloods called Métis, the offspring of intermarriage between local Indians and French and English trappers, lived scattered throughout the prairies and the northwest. As for the Indians themselves, no one had ever accurately gauged their numbers.

The Métis caused the first difficulty: When surveyors arrived at the Red River in advance of a new influx of pioneers, the Métis banded together to defend their ancestral rights. Under the leadership of a charismatic young man called Louis Riel, the Métis rose in a brief but fierce rebellion that was harshly suppressed by a federal government intent on creating the new province of Manitoba.

In the aftermath of the troubles, Riel fled across the border to Montana, to live quietly until his people called on him once more. The Métis rebels dispersed westward, toward the Saskatchewan River. The troops who had opposed them also departed, leaving behind a void of authority. Even the modest law and order imposed by Louis Riel's men had vanished, and Manitoba—indeed, the whole expanse of Rupert's Land—was wide open to every kind of abuse.

The main victims were the Indians. Unscrupulous whisky traders—many of them tough and ruthless veterans of the American Civil War—threatened to wash whole tribes away in floods of cheap liquor. Worse still, overhunting had brought close to extinction the buffalo herds on which the Indians depended, while smallpox and tuberculosis raged unchecked.

By 1873, even Macdonald, never a man to take precipitate action, agreed that the situation was intolerable. To bring the rule of law to the wilderness, Canada raised a body of armed men who went on to become one of the world's legendary constabularies: the North West Mounted Police.

Their very appearance was enough to scare off the whisky traders, who had no stomach for a big fight, and the relationship the Mounties generally struck up with the Indians saved countless lives. As the Indian wars across the border in the United States grew more bitter, the Mounties' red coats proved a tremendous psychological asset: When whole refugee Indian nations crossed the "Medicine Line" into Canada to escape the hated blue of the U.S. Cavalry, they would usually surrender peaceably to a handful of troopers whose dress was scarlet.

Yet, sadly for the Indians, the Mounties did not create the laws they enforced. The loyalty of the government in Ottawa was to the settlers already flooding westward. By the late 1880s, Indians were being corraled on reservations and sent to schools to learn the ways of the white man. Their rights to tribal lands were often ignored or violated, leaving a legacy of bitterness, which exploded in the native-rights movement of the 1970s.

Above all, though, the Mounties brought law and order to the expanding Canadian frontier: From the 1870s onward, there was no gun law of the kind familiar south of the border. It was a rare exercise in moral authority rather than one imposed by physical force, for the Mounties were always ex-

2

iguously few. Not the least of their achievements was in the icy Yukon Territory, where gold was discovered near the Klondike River in 1896. Thousands of hopefuls poured in from all over the world, expecting to strike it rich amid the awe-inspiring glaciers; the Mounties had to stop the gold-crazed newcomers from killing not only each other but also themselves out of sheer stupidity. Mounties patrolled wilderness trails to keep an eye out for lost tenderfeet as well as attending to police duties in Dawson, a collection of shacks, brothels, and saloons that was the Yukon's only town. They served not just as law enforcers but also as postmen, medical workers, and the nearest thing the region was to know to a welfare service, all for less than a dollar's pay a day.

In the meantime, work continued on the transcontinental railroad. By 1876, however, it extended only from Halifax to Quebec and, despite the federal government's promises, its progress westward remained slow. In 1880, the newly constituted Canadian Pacific Railway Company took over the job of constructing the western section. Although its finances were constantly precarious, the railroad pushed ahead across the Canadian Shield and the Rockies. By 1885, only a few small gaps remained in the 2,920 miles of rail linking Montreal and Vancouver in far-off British Columbia, and large stretches of the track were already being put to use by westward-bound settlers.

But 1885 was to be an unhappy year. The mixed-blood Métis, pushed from the province of Manitoba 15 years before by the homesteaders, were now under threat in their last great enclave on the Saskatchewan. Desperate, they summoned their old leader from his Montana retreat.

Louis Riel had lost neither his charisma nor his dedication to his people. To begin with, he organized peaceful resistance and petitioned for a bill of rights by which Ottawa would recognize Métis land claims. But the government's lack of response, growing Métis discontent, and Riel's own sense of mission soon combined to push him outside the law: In March 1885, he formed the Provisional Government of the Saskatchewan and offered the local Mountie detachment the choice of either surrendering, with a safe-conduct out of Métis territory, or waging "a war of extermination upon all those who have shown themselves hostile to our rights." An attempt at negotiation ended in a nasty firefight that the Métis sharpshooters had no trouble winning. The Mounties withdrew, and for a time, Riel controlled the Saskatchewan.

The government reacted to the success of the Métis with near panic. With the new railroad largely in place, 8,000 troops were rushed to the scene, complete with artillery and newfangled Gatling guns. Métis marksmanship and knowledge of the ground, coupled with the egregious bungling of the federal commanders, inflicted painful casualties on the expeditionary force, but in the end the rebels were overwhelmed by sheer numbers.

Riel was captured and charged with high treason. To his disgust, his defense lawyers tried to have him acquitted on grounds of insanity. "I cannot abandon my dignity," he declared. A jury found him guilty, however, and although it entered a plea for clemency, he was sentenced to death. Louis Riel had been his people's messiah; now, through the weeks of appeals that followed, he was its most public sacrifice. French Canada, not surprisingly, lent

him its passionate support. "History will reserve a glorious page for you," applauded one French newspaper. But English-speaking Canada thirsted for revenge: At least 80 volunteers had died fighting Riel's Métis, and Ontario had neither forgotten nor forgiven the 1870 revolt. "He shall hang, though every dog in Quebec bark in his favor," declared Macdonald, once more in power after a Liberal interlude. And hanged he was, on November 16, 1885, amid bitter feelings that have persisted for more than a century.

Only nine days before Riel's execution, the last spike was driven in the Canadian Pacific Railway. It was not a gaudy ceremony. The company's hardheaded, U.S.-born chief engineer, William Van Horne, wanted no American-style jamboree. "The last spike will be just as good an iron one as there is between Montreal and Vancouver," he insisted. "And anyone who wants to see it driven will have to pay full fare." An unbroken line of railroad track at last linked the Atlantic and Pacific coasts. Surely now Canada was a nation.

Yet in the aftermath of Riel's death, the French-English division seemed set to become a gaping wound. The political problem was worsened by the general world recession of the time, exacerbated in Canada's case by high tariff walls erected by the United States, its greatest potential trading partner. Canada responded by adopting protectionist measures of its own. John A. Macdonald's national policy built up the machine shops and factories of Toronto and Montreal but forced western farmers, then busy turning the new Prairie Provinces into an ocean of wheat, to pay more for their farm machinery than if they had been able to

AN EMPIRE FOUNDED ON FUR

Fur traders gather at Upper Fort Garry, a Hudson's Bay Company outpost established in 1822 on a site close to the present-day city of Winnipeg. At such settlements, company officers supervised the affairs of an organization whose monopoly covered nearly half the nation.

Founded in 1670 by royal charter, the Hudson's Bay Company (HBC) was set up to exploit the European demand for fur, principally the beaver pelts used for men's hats. By the terms of its indenture, the company was given sole trading rights over roughly 1.4 million square miles of largely unexplored land.

At first the French settlers challenged the claims, but after the French defeat at Quebec in 1759, traders of the rival North West Company became its main competitors. Tensions between them led to the Red River Massacre of 1816, when 21 HBC employees were killed by men of the opposing company.

After the firms merged in 1821, the HBC dominated the fur trade and imposed law and order in its territories. From 1869, though, when it sold lands to the Crown, it became purely commercial. Today the HBC, Canada's largest retailer, is prominent in the fur business and has extensive mineral holdings.

CHRONOLOGY OF KEY EVENTS

c. 10,000 B.C. A land bridge across the Bering Strait allows Ice Age hunters, the ancestors of today's Indians and Inuit, to migrate from Siberia to North America. Both societies evolve complex, semino-madic cultures.

c. 1000 A.D. Viking adventurers reach today's Nova Scotia and Newfoundland. A short-lived settlement is established.

1497 John Cabot claims Labrador and Newfoundland for Henry VII of England. His descriptions of the abundant cod of the Grand Banks win the attention of European fishermen.

1534-1535 French mariner Jacques Cartier *(below)* explores the St. Lawrence River system.

1541 Cartier returns with colonists to found New France. The colony fails.

1605 French settlers led by Samuel de Champlain and his patron, the Sieur de Monts, build Port Royal in Nova Scotia, which they name Acadia.

1608 Champlain builds a fort at Quebec to advance the fur trade. With Indian help, he and his *coureurs de bois* (woodsmen) explore the hinterland.

1610-1611 English explorer Henry Hudson charts Hudson Bay. English settlers arrive in Newfoundland.

1625 Jesuit missionaries arrive in Quebec and begin working among the Huron Indians.

1629 The first British settlement in Nova Scotia is founded.

1642 French pioneers found Montreal. Iroquois Indians harass the settlement mercilessly for 20 years.

1663 Louis XIV of France declares New France to be a royal province. Troops are sent to defend the colony, and further settlement is encouraged.

1670 The Hudson's Bay Company *(coat of arms, right)* is set up by royal charter in London. Britain's King Charles II grants the fur-trading monopoly 1.35 million square miles of wilderness.

1689-1748 A succession of Anglo-French wars in Europe extend across the Atlantic. Neither side prevails, although the French cede Acadia (except for Cape Breton Island) to the British by the Treaty of Utrecht in 1713.

1731-1744 The French explorer Pierre de la Vérendrye extends the French chain of fur-trading posts as far as the Saskatchewan River.

1754 Anthony Henday, a Hudson's Bay Company trader, reaches the Rockies. The outbreak of the French and Indian War in North America renews Anglo-French hostilities.

1759 The British under General Wolfe capture Quebec.

1760 Montreal surrenders to the British.

1763 The Treaty of Paris assigns all North America east of the Mississippi to the British. France retains only St. Pierre and Miquelon, islands off the Newfoundland coast.

1774 The Quebec Act guarantees respect for the French language and civil law, as well as for the Roman Catholic Church.

later, George Vancouver—a midshipman on Cook's expedition—returns and circumnavigates the island that now bears his name.

1791 The Constitutional Act divides the old French colony in two. Lower Canada—today's Quebec—remains a French enclave; Upper Canada—now Ontario—is overwhelmingly English-speaking. Both are granted some representative government, as are the Maritime colonies of Nova Scotia, New Brunswick, and Prince Edward Island.

1793 A team under the leadership of Alexander Mackenzie become the first explorers to reach the Pacific Ocean by an overland route.

1812-1814 War breaks out between the United States and Britain. A U.S. invasion fails to overwhelm Canada.

1815 With the end of the Napoleonic Wars in Europe, Canada receives its first large-scale British immigration.

1775-1783 During the American War of Independence, Canada sides with Britain; thousands of refugee Empire Loyalists move to the colony.

1778 Britain's Captain James Cook explores the Pacific coast. Fourteen years

1830 Searching for the Northwest Passage, Scottish explorer Captain John Ross reaches the Boothia Peninsula, encountering Inuit on the way *(above)*.

1837 Agitation for representative government leads to rebellion in Upper and

Lower Canada. The uprisings are crushed, but Britain sends Lord Durham to find the cause of discontent.

1839 The Durham Report recommends reuniting Upper and Lower Canada and increased autonomy for the colonies.

1841 Canada becomes one colony.

1896 The Klondike Gold Rush begins. Sir Wilfred Laurier becomes Canada's first French-speaking prime minister. His 15-year rule coincides with a massive immigration of Europeans.

1899-1902 Canadian troops fight alongside the British in the South African (Boer) War.

1956 Canada opposes Anglo-French intervention in the Suez Canal, and Prime Minister Lester Pearson's peace plan is adopted by the United Nations.

1967 Montreal hosts EXPO 67 (*Habitat building, below*) to celebrate Canada's centenary. General de Gaulle, on a state visit, issues a call for a "free Quebec."

1968 Pierre Trudeau becomes prime minister. Réné Lévesque, a Quebec television journalist, forms the Parti Québécois to press for a separate Francophone state.

1970 Terrorists of the Quebec Liberation Front kidnap a British diplomat and a government minister. Trudeau responds with the War Measures Act.

1976 Lévesque's Parti Québécois wins the

1848 Canada and Nova Scotia are granted local governing power; Newfoundland, Prince Edward Island, and New Brunswick gain the same rights in 1855.

1858 The Crown Colony of British Columbia is created on the Pacific seaboard. It is united with the colony of Vancouver Island eight years later.

1867 By the British North America Act, Quebec, Ontario, New Brunswick, and Nova Scotia join together to form the self-governing Dominion of Canada.

1869 The Hudson's Bay Company sells its vast territory to Canada for $300,000. Métis trappers rebel unsuccessfully when Canada's westward expansion threatens their way of life.

1870 The new province of Manitoba, formerly part of the old Hudson's Bay Company domain, joins the Dominion.

1871 British Columbia federates.

1873 The North West Mounted Police are set up to bring order to Canada's lawless frontier. Prince Edward Island federates.

1885 Led by Louis Riel, the Métis of the Saskatchewan River stage another armed uprising. After a series of wilderness battles, Riel is captured and hanged. In November, the last spike of the Canadian Pacific Railway is driven in (*above*), completing the first overland route across the continent.

1905 The new provinces of Alberta and Saskatchewan join the Dominion.

1914-1918 Canada loses more than 60,000 lives fighting at Britain's side during World War I.

1919 Canada signs the Versailles peace treaty as a nation in its own right.

1921 William Lyon Mackenzie King becomes prime minister. He is to dominate Canadian politics for 27 years.

1931 By the Statute of Westminster, Canada, along with the other British dominions, gains complete autonomy.

1933 In the depths of the Great Depression, unemployment levels reach 25 percent.

1939-1945 World War II costs more than 40,000 Canadian lives but makes the country into an industrial power.

1947 Alberta's first oil pipeline inaugurates the exploitation of the province's huge energy resources.

1949 Canada joins the North Atlantic Treaty Organization (NATO). Newfoundland enters the Dominion as Canada's 10th province.

1950 Canada fights in the Korean War.

1954 Construction of the U.S.-Canadian early warning defense system begins.

Quebec provincial elections. The Olympic Games are staged in Montreal.

1980 Lévesque holds a referendum on the separatist issue; Quebec votes to stay inside federal Canada.

1982 By the Constitution Act, the British Parliament surrenders its power over the Canadian Constitution. A Charter of Rights and Freedoms guarantees human rights.

1987 The Meech Lake Accord, agreed to by Mulroney and representatives of all 10 provinces, officially recognizes Quebec's uniqueness and strengthens the Canadian federation.

1988 In January, a free-trade treaty that, by 1999, will eliminate tariffs between the world's two largest trading partners is sent to the U.S. Congress and Canada's House of Commons.

buy it direct from the Americans. Western resentment toward eastern economic dominance became a theme of Canadian politics in the 1880s and has remained so.

The situation changed enormously for the better after 1896, when a new Liberal party-led government, headed by Wilfred Laurier, the country's first French-Canadian premier, took power. Laurier himself represented the spirit of compromise on which the nation's survival depended. An orator fluent in both languages, he had an enviable knack of inspiring confidence among English Canadians. But the real reason for the improvement was less Laurier's considerable political acumen than the mysterious workings of the world economy, which entered a period of great and sustained expansion.

Between the early 1890s and 1914, a small-town society that had built modest wealth on timber and wheat transformed itself into a big-city industrial power. Soon smoking foundries, shoe factories, and cotton mills lined Montreal's Lachine Canal; steelworks, machine shops, and factories of all sorts stretched in an unbroken line around the western rim of Lake Ontario from Hamilton to Toronto. The whole of

Canada, from Victoria, British Columbia, to Halifax, Nova Scotia, ended up buying its industrial goods from this central Canadian industrial core.

With the surging economic growth came a new urban working class, many of them immigrants, working long, dangerous hours and living in rickety wooden tenements. Canada, which in the past had always prided itself on avoiding the social ills of Europe and its neighbor to the south, now had problems of its own: woefully inadequate schools, sanitation, housing, and recreation for a new population that was pounding out the nation's wealth. The first Canadian labor unions and social welfare institutions were founded at this time to meet the challenge.

Immigration to the Prairie Provinces also increased enormously. For the first time, a substantial proportion of the immigrants were not from Britain, which could no longer provide enough of the kind of people Canada required. Laurier's interior minister summed up the requirements well: "I think a stalwart peasant in a sheepskin coat, born on the soil, whose forefathers have been farmers for generations, with a stout wife and a half-dozen children, is good quality." Huge numbers of the

stalwarts the minister described came from the poverty-stricken plains of Eastern Europe: Ukrainians, Poles, and Hungarians, including many Jews.

The new provinces of Alberta and Saskatchewan were formed in 1905; the population continued to swell, with 2.5 million newcomers arriving between 1896 and 1913. But trouble was on the horizon. Laurier lost the 1911 election, partly because some Canadians (mostly English) feared that his free-trade policies with the United States would allow the Americans to swallow up Canadian independence, and partly because other Canadians (mostly French) were convinced that his attempt to build a Canadian navy for imperial defense meant a sacrifice of independence to Britain. "I am branded in Quebec as a traitor to the French," he said despairingly, "and in Ontario as a traitor to the English. I am neither. I am a Canadian." When World War I broke out in 1914, Canadians missed his leadership.

The constitutional situation in 1914 brought Canada automatically into the war at Britain's side. As a whole, the nation fought willingly enough. Even though few French Canadians had much desire to lay down their lives for

In a contemporary sketch drawn in 1824, the governor of the Red River Colony begins a journey 13 years after his domain was established on land formerly owned by the Hudson's Bay Company. The territory joined Canada in 1870 as part of Manitoba.

the British Empire—or, indeed, for Britain's ally, France—volunteers enlisted by the hundreds of thousands. The Canadians earned a formidable reputation as fighters—so much so that they were used again and again as assault troops, suffering casualties to match. By the war's end, Canada had lost more than 60,000 from a population of only nine million.

On the Somme, at Vimy Ridge, in the crowning horror of Passchendaele, Canada's soldiers bought their battle honors with blood. But the high casualty rate caused Prime Minister Robert Borden's government to introduce conscription in 1917 as a way of replenishing the ranks. The resulting outrage of French Canada badly damaged national unity.

Fortunately, the war ended in the following year, before the division became unbridgeable. In its aftermath, Canada had a first opportunity to appear on the international stage: The country's dead had paid for a place on the treaty-making councils and a seat in the new League of Nations. The war and its cost also did much to weaken the old British connection. Canada's support for the empire could no longer be counted on as automatic.

The British, anxious to retain at least a memory of their imperial dreams, found in 1926 a face-saving formula. Canada, with Australia, New Zealand, South Africa, Newfoundland—then still a separate entity—and Britain itself, would be "autonomous communities within the British Empire, equal in status, in no way subordinate to one another in any aspect of their domestic or external affairs, though united by a common allegiance to the Crown and freely associated as members of the British Commonwealth of Nations."

This masterpiece of vagueness was solemnized by the Statute of Westminster in 1931; just how it might be interpreted remained to be seen.

In 1921, the Liberal party had come to power under a new leader, William Lyon Mackenzie King, grandson of the 1837 rebel and one of the chief architects of the new, decentralized British Empire. A master compromiser, respected at least grudgingly by both Canadian communities, he went on to establish an astonishing record of political longevity. Save for a brief interval in the mid-1920s and a five-year gap in the 1930s, he remained prime minister until 1948. A small, pudgy man with a genius for colorless circumlocution in his public speeches, Mackenzie King concealed in his private life a strange secret: He used spirit mediums to commune with his dead mother, and few major decisions were taken without her advice. His political success, however, was built on firmer

A controversial figure in Canadian history, Louis Riel led two rebellions by Métis—French-speaking descendants of mixed blood. After a first defeat in 1870, Riel took refuge in the United States. He took up arms again in 1885, but after two months' fighting was captured and executed.

ground—on a shrewd awareness that Canadians had little taste for ideological politics. Hence he was both a champion of free enterprise and a pioneer of Canadian labor legislation, an isolationist in the 1930s and an internationalist during and after World War II, an architect of the modern welfare state, and a man who believed in low taxes and firm economic management.

He also had the good fortune—as it turned out—to be out of power during the worst of the Great Depression of the 1930s, and the blame for Canada's troubles fell on the hapless Conservative party member R. B. Bennett. The Depression hit Canada hard. Prices for its primary products of wheat, timber, and minerals plummeted on world markets; the effect was to turn once-booming mining communities in northern Ontario into ghost towns. For thousands of western farming families, the homesteading dream turned into a nightmare of bankruptcy and eviction forced by bank foreclosures. The effect of years of drought, combined with the erosion of the once-rich prairie topsoil caused by poorly fertilized "wheat mining," had turned all their holdings into dust bowls.

In this time of social ferment and economic crisis, Bennett's government tried desperately to adapt U.S. President Franklin Roosevelt's New Deal strategy to Canadian conditions, with programs of public works and economic pump-priming measures. It is to the Depression decade, to both the Bennett and Mackenzie King governments, that Canada owes its distinctive balance between state and private enterprise, with the creation of the state-owned Canadian Broadcasting System and Trans Canada Airline (which has since been renamed Air Canada), and the publicly

GOLD FEVER ON THE KLONDIKE

Laden with supplies, would-be gold prospectors trudge up the Chilkoot Pass, a daunting obstacle on the overland trail to the Klondike goldfields. Even using steps cut in the ice, heavily burdened men could take six hours to climb the last 1,000 feet, which sloped at 45 degrees.

Canada has several gold rushes in its history, but none captured the national imagination like the converging of 100,000 hopefuls on the frozen Klondike River between 1897 and 1898. Mostly, they found only hardship and disillusion. Although some gold could be found on the surface or panned from the river, the bulk lay in bedrock under at least 16 feet of frozen soil, which first had to be thawed. The lucky few who struck it rich were often the prey of con men and prostitutes in Dawson, a town of 30,000 that grew up almost overnight at the mouth of the Klondike.

By 1899, the diggings had been almost worked out, having yielded $50 million (Canadian) of gold—about what the prospectors were estimated to have spent getting to the fields. However, the gold rush was the catalyst of a chain of mineral discoveries that have changed the face of the Canadian Far North.

A prospector pans for gold, using a sluice box to separate the metal from river gravel.

Prospectors crowd Dawson's main street at the height of the gold rush.

owned hydroelectric power companies.

Canadians of the 1930s watched the rise of Hitler in Germany, and the inexorable slide into conflict, with painful memories of World War I. Yet when war in Europe finally erupted in September 1939, Canada was involved almost at once. Ever since the Statute of Westminster, there had been legal arguments about the possible neutrality of Canada in a future war involving Britain; Mackenzie King, back in power, waited a week before joining Britain's declaration of war on Germany, thus adroitly asserting the principle of neutrality without abandoning Britain by putting that principle into practice.

The human costs once more were terrible. The abortive Dieppe Raid in 1942 was almost exclusively a Canadian tragedy; the nation's vital role in the Normandy invasion and in the bomber offensive over Germany added a long list of names to the memorials of 1914-1918 and put a heavy strain on human resources. Mindful of events in 1917, Mackenzie King resisted conscription as long as possible. In 1944, when the toll of Canadian troops fighting their way through France necessitated some degree of compulsory service, even Quebec recognized that Mackenzie King had done his best. There was loud protest, but Quebec votes ensured that Mackenzie King won the 1945 elections that followed the German surrender.

Canada emerged from the war, somewhat to Canadians' surprise, as the world's fourth-largest industrial power—quite an achievement for a country with a population of fewer than 20 million. But the investment that had made the country's rapid expansion possible was largely American, and the control of many Canadian industries was in American hands. Cana-

dians began to ask themselves whether they had in fact merely passed through nationhood as a brief interval in a long history as a colony—first of Britain, then of the United States.

Close defense links—not only membership in NATO but also in the NORAD organization for North American air defense, which puts much of the Royal Canadian Air Force under American command—further underlined Canadian dependence on its neighbor. But it has never been a servile ally: Canada pointedly retained trading links with Fidel Castro's Cuba, and diplomatic links—and lucrative grain deals—with Communist China.

The period from 1945 to 1965 was perhaps the golden age of Canadian diplomacy, crowned by Prime Minister Lester Pearson's Nobel Peace prize in 1956 for peacemaking efforts in the aftermath of the Middle East War. In the course of that conflict, Canada solidly opposed both its mother countries,

Britain and France, for their intervention over Suez. During the Vietnam War, Canada tried to urge restraint on the American government, only to learn to its embarrassment that its neighbor to the south had little patience for well-meant advice from across the border. Since then, Canadian foreign policy has put the country in the forefront of UN peace-keeping missions in the world's trouble spots and has promoted attempts to improve relations between developed and underdeveloped countries.

The background to the upswing in Canadian diplomatic activity was a spell of unprecedented prosperity at home. For 20 years after the end of World War II, Canada enjoyed a virtually continuous boom. Alberta's first oil field came on line in 1947; and the stubborn old colony of Newfoundland at last joined the federation in 1949 as the dominion's 10th province. A new wave of more than two million immigrants

from Italy, Greece, Poland, Hungary, and Asia radically altered the complexion of many Canadian cities. And people grew steadily richer. As in the United States, the 1950s were the golden age of suburbia. Canadians became accustomed to a new kind of North American life-style, based on the car; the superhighway; the shopping center; the fast-food restaurant; and the suburban single-family home with its backyard, its family room, and its ever-glowing TV screen.

The most startling developments of the time, though, occurred in Quebec. Already in the 1940s, a fledgling labor-union movement, backed by progressive young priests and intellectuals (among them the future prime minister, Pierre Elliott Trudeau), had begun to challenge the powers that held Quebec society immobile: the Catholic church, the English business elite, and the political machine of the wily, corrupt, often despotic Quebecois Premier Maurice Duplessis.

Duplessis's death in 1960 proved a turning point. With the arrival in power of the Liberal administration of Jean Lesage, the process of change, since dubbed the Quiet Revolution, got under way. The transformation of Quebec society was dramatic. Birthrates plunged, and control of the school system was largely wrested from the Catholic church. Politically, the Lesage administration succeeded in winning a large measure of autonomy from the federal government with respect to language, culture, and education. A schism subsequently developed within the Quebecois ranks between those who wanted Quebec to develop within a redefined Canadian federalism and others who sought total independence for the province. Réné Lévesque founded the Parti Québécois (PQ) in 1968 to further the latter aim peacefully, but there were other separatists who were less fussy about their methods. The first bombs of a sporadic terrorist campaign had exploded in Montreal in 1963.

The political climate was already tense when the federal government, in 1967, threw what was in essence a gigantic birthday party to celebrate its centenary—the 1967 World's Fair in Montreal. EXPO 67 was the culminating moment of postwar Canadian national sentiment: an exultant celebration of a young country's pride in its achievement, which drew millions of Canadian families across the land in a pilgrimage to its beautiful and imaginative pavilions. At the same time, however, EXPO 67 occurred at the high

point of the Quebec cultural and nationalist explosion. One of the guests of honor, France's General Charles de Gaulle, chose the opportunity for a speech of calculated insult to English Canada. From the balcony of Montreal's city hall de Gaulle deliberately took up the separatist rallying call, *"Vive le Québec libre!"* ("Long live free Quebec!") De Gaulle was not invited back, and a chill enveloped Franco-Canadian relations.

Not all French Canadians were separatists, however. In 1968, Pierre Trudeau emerged as Liberal party leader and federal prime minister. Single, bilingual, youthful in attitude, and a millionaire, Trudeau proved to be one of the most colorful leaders in Canada's history. He won the 1968 election on a strongly pro-Federation stand and in

1969 got an act through Parliament making French the second official language for all of Canada.

Despite this gesture, Lévesque's popularity increased in Quebec, and so did the activities of the extremists. In 1970, the so-called Quebec Liberation Front (FLQ) kidnapped a British diplomat and Quebec's minister of labor, holding the two officials to ransom against demands for money and the release of previously imprisoned FLQ members. Trudeau invoked the War Measures Act, giving his government dramatic powers and flooding the province with troops. Such drastic action impressed most voters and helped save the diplomat, but the luckless minister was murdered. The majority of French Canadians were appalled by the outrage, and the PQ suffered a setback.

A *Punch* cartoon honors Canadian soldiers for their role in the Ypres campaign of 1915.

A NATION TEMPERED IN TWO WORLD WARS

Canada earned its battle honors in both world wars, fighting with Britain. A total of 1,117,000 Canadians, most of them volunteers, took part on the battlefields of Ypres and Vimy Ridge, Sicily, and Normandy. More than 100,000 died.

Besides strengthening the Allied forces, Canada made huge contributions of war matériel, much of it shipped to Europe via the hazardous trans-Atlantic route from Halifax, Nova Scotia.

For its sacrifices in World War I, Canada was present at the Versailles Peace Conference. World War II confirmed the country's status as a "middle power," while the economy benefited from industrial efforts made on the Allies' behalf.

As the 1970s progressed, Quebec separatism became less an issue because of the greater problems the federal government faced. The economy was in difficulty and unemployment was rising. Pollution was also a major concern: Acid rain and runoff produced by U.S. as well as Canadian industries was destroying Ontario's lakes. Furthermore, oil and mineral discoveries in the north and west were encouraging the western provinces to demand more autonomy. When Lévesque at last won control of Quebec province in the 1976 elections, it seemed that Canada might disintegrate completely.

For four tense years, Lévesque held the threat of a separatist referendum over the federal government, while Trudeau wore himself out in an effort to hold his country together. By the 1979 federal elections, Trudeau was a shadow of his former self: He lost and later resigned the Liberal leadership. But the lackluster Conservative administration replacing him fell after nine months. Trudeau bounded back from retirement to win a stunning victory in 1980, just in time to see Lévesque's hopes crushed as the Quebecois voted no in the long-awaited referendum.

Trudeau returned to power with a specific goal in mind, one that had haunted him since his first entry into politics in the 1960s. He wanted to remove the mandate that amendments to the Canadian Constitution could be ratified only by act of the British Parliament—a residue of the colonial period that had survived only because of disagreement among Canadians as to what should replace it. At the same time, the prime minister was determined to attach to the Constitution a written bill of rights that would spell out citizens' standing vis-à-vis the state

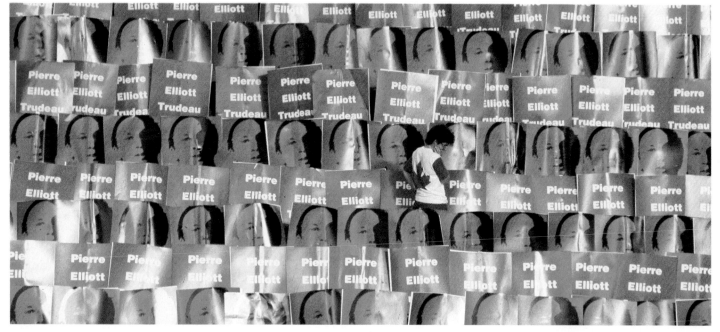

At the 1968 Liberal party convention, a campaign worker considers posters promoting Pierre Trudeau. A few weeks later, Trudeau became prime minister; with one nine-month break, he would continue in office for 15 years—longer than any other major Western leader of his day.

and would guarantee fundamental liberties; previously, the citizens of Canada—following the British lead—had looked for protection to the uncodified decisions of the common law. The latter proposal in particular generated hostility in the provincial legislatures, where many considered it an unwarranted federal interference in the running of their affairs.

Trudeau, however, considered patriation, as the process was christened, to be his political testament; he set about pushing it through against all opposition. And in 1982, Trudeau succeeded in his mission; Her Majesty's Parliament in Westminster passed the Constitution Act, enabling amendments to the Canadian Constitution, as spelled out in the British North America Act of 1867, to be passed in Canada alone. To address the issue of whether provinces should have the right to veto

amendments proposed by the federal government, a compromise formula was worked out. All amendments would require federal consent plus approval by the legislatures of at least two thirds of the 10 provinces, with a proviso that those two thirds must contain between them 50 percent of the population of Canada. The so-called Charter of Rights and Freedoms was attached to the act.

The successful passage of patriation was Trudeau's last victory. The year the measure passed, 1982, saw Canada in the depths of its worst slump since the Great Depression, with 1 worker in 8 out of a job and interest rates soaring above 20 percent. The prime minister, it seemed, had lost his way. Never popular in the western provinces, he was now judged by the nation at large on the country's lackluster economic performance and was found wanting. He

finally stepped down in 1984, just 80 days before his Liberal party suffered crushing defeat by the Progressive Conservatives under Brian Mulroney, a bilingual labor lawyer from Montreal.

Nevertheless, Pierre Elliott Trudeau had left a legacy whose significance would only increase with the passing of time, as the full implications of the Charter of Rights and Freedoms made themselves felt in the courts. Patriation, too, had a long-term significance; Canada was for the first time a fully sovereign state.

An earlier prime minister, Wilfred Laurier, once said: "The 20th century belongs to Canada." This has echoed ironically through the years, for Canada's progress has not been as glorious as Laurier predicted. Nonetheless, Canadians still hold on to those feelings of pride, hope, and optimism as the century draws to its close.

71

Settlers traveling westward from Montreal while away the journey in one of the Canadian Pacific's so-called colonist sleeping cars.

WE'RE SAILING WEST, WE'RE SAILING WEST,
TO PRAIRIE LANDS SUNKISSED AND BLEST—
THE CROFTER'S TRAIL TO HAPPINESS.

Leaving Britain for a new life in Canada at the turn of
the century, an emigrant family endorses a Canadian-
government slogan designed to attract agricultural settlers.

PIONEERS OF THE PRAIRIES

To the underprivileged of 19th-century Europe, the Canadian West offered a dream of independence and honestly won wealth. Its vast, virtually unpeopled spaces seemed ideal for wheat farming. And in 1885, the territory became easily accessible too: The completion of the Canadian Pacific Railway in that year meant that the long westward journey—six months' haul by wagon train—was reduced to about a week. It was not surprising that once the supply of good farmland in the western United States began to dwindle, the trickle of immigrants into Canada's wilds became a flood. Between 1900 and 1913, about 2.5 million settlers arrived.

The Canadian government took energetic steps to foster the dream, for it was keen to exploit the natural resources of the prairie regions and secure them against inroads from the United States. A publicity organization was created to solicit homesteaders with such incentives as cheap land and streamlined immigration procedures, as well as subsidized steamship fares across the Atlantic. But the tickets that were offered were to a hard and lonely life. The newcomers had to struggle with backbreaking toil in an unfamiliar and sometimes forbidding climate, and the rudimentary fabric of a simple society was slow to take shape around them.

In the prerailroad days of the 1870s, teams of oxen—slower but cheaper than horses—pull the wagons of settlers making their way westward.

The plowed line of a firebreak—an indispensable precaution against destructive prairie conflagrations—surrounds a homesteading family's cabin. As

Snow buries a homesteader's barn in Saskatchewan after a blizzard. In winter, temperatures on the prairies routinely fell to a bitter 3° F.

ondition of taking up the government's concessionary land grant—160 acres for $10—settlers had to build a house within three years.

A farmer's wife draws water for her two cows from the well dug on her homestead. Women in the settler communities led a hard and busy life firmly within the traditional female role: They managed the house and kitchen gardens, fed the animals and the family, and reared children.

An immigrant couple and their little girl welcome neighbors to a family meal in the cramped living room of their farm near Edmonton in Alberta. The large number of single men attracted to the West meant that for many years men far outnumbered women among the settlers.

In the autumn of 1898, the crew operating a steam-driven threshing machine takes a short break. The thresher traveled from farm to farm at harvesttime to process the wheat crop on which all members of the community depended for their survival—and their hoped-for prosperity.

Near the town of Viking in Alberta, a communal mailbox perched on rickety legs serves a group of homesteaders too remote for regular deliveries. Many poorer settlers were isolated from towns and the all-important railroad because the rail company owned most of the land bordering it.

In 1906, a rough cabin is the temporary quarters of a Vegreville, Alberta, bank. Although land was virtually free, homesteaders found that profits could be slow to come. Animals and equipment often cost them all their savings, and many were soon heavily in debt to financial institutions.

Pairs of warm durable gloves—vital in the harsh Canadian winter—festoon a general store in Wetaskiwin, south of Edmonton. As the population of the prairie states mushroomed, so their communities grew in size and sophistication: Edmonton had 70,000 inhabitants by the mid-teens.

3

An array of portraits reflecting Canada's ethnic diversity includes an Inuit woman *(top, center)* and a Chinese girl *(center)*. Sometimes dress proclaims an allegiance: Tartans advertise Scottish ancestry *(top, left)*, while a French-Canadian girl's T-shirt indicates her province *(bottom, right)*.

A MOSAIC OF PEOPLES

Modern Canada prides itself on being a multicultural society—not so much a melting pot as a kaleidoscope of peoples who have retained many of their distinctive ethnic characteristics and yet have learned to live together in harmony and mutual goodwill. The country even has a minister for multiculturalism, who is responsible for promoting the interests of the nation's 30-odd ethnic constituents. Yet the greater part of these ethnic groups conforms to a recognizable North American life-style and is more or less assimilated with one of the two main divisions, the British and the French Canadians, but usually with the former.

Politically and economically, the dominant segment of Canadian society is still one that stems from an English-speaking background, though in the 1980s it comprised only 40 percent of the population. To call its members English Canadian would be a misnomer, since they include a conspicuous number of people of Scottish, Irish, and Welsh extraction, as well as descendants of Empire Loyalists who left the United States for Canada after the Revolutionary War.

To picture the life-style typical of Anglophone Canada, then, imagine a family that traces its heritage back to Scotland; call them the Bells. Like 85 percent of Canadians, the Bells would reside within 200 miles of the U.S. border. The Bells have two children and live in a three- or four-bedroom house in a suburb of, say, Toronto; but the Bells could equally well live outside Vancouver or Winnipeg. There are two cars in the garage, one of which Mr. Bell drives to his job as a foreman in a paper-products factory.

Mrs. Bell devotes her full time to being a wife and mother; she does not have a salaried job outside the home. She uses the other car to go shopping and to chauffeur the children to and from their sports practice or piano lessons after school and on weekends. Molly, the family's Labrador retriever, often rides in the back seat. On Fridays, Mrs. Bell has her hair done by Sonya, the Czech hairdresser who runs a beauty-salon-cum-neighborhood- gossip establishment at the shopping center not far from the Bells' home.

The family is comfortably off but by no means rich; the house is heavily mortgaged and needs repainting. Not long ago, major repairs to the central-heating system nearly depleted the Bells' savings account. In this, as in many respects, they are probably quite similar to an equivalent family in the United States.

Yet there are elements of both style and substance that make the Bells distinctively Canadian. For one thing, they pay proportionately more taxes but also receive more benefits, especially in the field of health care. Last year, when Mr. Bell had a bout of pneumonia, all his expenses were covered by federal Medicare and provincial medical insur ance. By and large, the Bells are better cushioned against economic shocks and unforeseen eventualities, thanks to Canadian social programs, substantial investment in insurance, and some of the world's most generous unemployment benefits. "We may live less well," Mr. Bell would concede, "but if we get into trouble we'll do better than if we lived in the United States."

The Bells and others like them have every reason to be glad to be living in Canada. Whereas in Britain they might still think of themselves as members of the working class, with a certain pride in that status but also with all the limitations in social mobility it entails, here they form part of a vast middle-income group that incorporates most of the population. In appearance, in aspiration, and even in accent, little would differentiate the Bells from most of their fellow Canadians.

But if class differences are muted in Canada, there are nonetheless large divergences to be found in income and hence in life-style. A sort of economic lift-off occurs somewhere in the professions, separating obviously affluent doctors, lawyers, engineers, and architects from median-income schoolteachers, civil servants, and owners of small businesses, as well as from skilled workers like the Bells. The majority of well-to-do Canadians will not flaunt their wealth, for that is not the Canadian style. Still, it is evidently there, in the discreetly elegant designer clothes, in the frequently renewed vacation tan, and in the two current-model cars in the garage. One of these vehicles may well be a station wagon, because its luggage space proves useful every summer when the family makes its annual trip to the lakeside cottage that serves as the family's vacation home.

The main residence may be a ranch-style house in the suburbs, with manicured lawns and flower beds tended with loving care by a Japanese gardening contractor; or, reflecting a present international yuppie trend, the family may have settled for a terrace house in a revitalized neighborhood downtown; the house will have been totally gutted and renovated, and its new status will be proclaimed by a big number plate of gleaming brass. Either way, the children will be driven each day to nursery school before going on to a public school or, if their parents are really wealthy, to one of the nation's small number of fee-paying private educational establishments. Almost invari-

ably they will then go on to college—an option not necessarily open to the Bells' children, for Canada is squeezed for places in higher education. Per capita, only two thirds as many Canadians as Americans go to college. Nonetheless, the nation has addressed the problem energetically since the 1960s; by the mid-1980s, 1 Canadian in 4 was going on to some form of post-secondary education as opposed to 1 in 10 in 1960.

Even upscale professionals, however, are not quite at the top of the heap in terms of wealth and comfort. Above them exists a very small subgroup of the superrich. In a trailblazing study published in 1965, *The Vertical Mosaic*, sociologist John Porter identified a key group of about 2,000 people who run the country's business and government, and it is from the ranks of this plutocracy that Canada's most privileged families are drawn. Here the perquisites that are enjoyed are the stuff of television soap operas: private planes, chauffeur-driven Rolls-Royces, polo ponies, as well as a landing strip for easy access to the ranch or farm that in this class replaces the lakeside cottage as a second home.

If the family has ties to old money, there may still be a hint of Britain in the family members' tone—it may be an old-fashioned look about their clothes, to indicate a sense of detachment from mere trendiness, or a vintage car gleamingly polished for the occasional country drive. But Canada has its new rich families, too, whose lack of reticence sometimes disconcerts their own compatriots. Their taste runs to flash, whether it be in the form of architect-designed townhouses with sunken living rooms and mirror-topped circular baths, vacation apartments on the beachfront in Maui or Miami, or in one

case reported by Canada's chronicler of the rich, Peter C. Newman, a bedroom ceiling decorated with $100,000 worth of gold leaf.

Such ostentation, the club members of Montreal or Toronto would maintain with a touch of anti-arriviste disdain, is found mainly in the west, among the property tycoons of Vancouver or the energy millionaires of Alberta. That province's boom town, Calgary, with a population of 625,000, became known as one of the growth cities that truly exemplifies the Canadian dream. Its residents owe their prosperity as much to oil and natural gas as to wheat and cattle, yet their annual fiesta, the Calgary Stampede, celebrates the cowboy-and-Indian mythology of the old frontier and focuses on such rodeo events as bucking broncos, the wild-horse race, steer wrestling, and chuckwagon racing. Virtually ev-

eryone in the city, including car salespeople and oil-company secretaries, puts on blue jeans, checked shirts, and ten-gallon hats for the duration of the Stampede; even the clergy are seen wearing Stetsons. Square dances are held in the streets, horses are hitched to the parking meters, and banks are redecorated to look like livery stables; and all the while, frontier music of uncertain vintage blares over a hundred loudspeakers.

The English-speaking Canadians who built this former North West Mounted Police post into a great city were no less adventurous than the pioneers who settled the American West, but the Canadians preferred to construct their lives and fortunes on the continuation of British principles and traditions. Often it was British money, supplied by far-sighted Scottish investment bankers, that financed the ranch-

es, mines, and oil wells. But in Alberta, everything happened on a scale undreamed of in congested Europe, where all the land was measured and parceled out in the Middle Ages. A Scots-Canadian lawyer, who came to Calgary before World World I and made the most of his opportunities to become a millionaire, caught this fact with a fine sense of understatement when he explained his success: "After making my way in ranching and mining for many years, I had a chance to buy oil exploration leases on eight million acres of very promising land." With some of his profits, he set up a foundation that endowed the city and province with art museums and ethnographic collections, but the undoubted apple of his eye was an equestrian statue of Robert the Bruce that he donated to Calgary for the enjoyment of its citizens, Scots or otherwise.

Like many of Canada's empire-builders, he equated "Canadianization" with Anglicization (or perhaps Caledonianization). Indeed, most of the Anglo-Scots take it for granted that it is their culture that others should emulate. In the higher strata of some Canadian cities, a kind of Olde English atmosphere is still assiduously cultivated. A few exclusive private schools continue, for instance, to instruct their pupils in cricket, a game that in Canada has the same sort of curiosity value as a 1936 Packard and draws inquisitive onlookers in a similar way. Afternoon tea at the Empress Hotel Tea Room in Victoria, British Columbia, also represents a splendid survival of Britishness left over from another age—although some Canadians have been known to mutter that this archaic ceremony is really staged for the benefit of the American tourists who come by ferry from

3

Seattle in order to experience the foreign thrill of an English tea. No one, however, would dare to say that the York Club in Toronto—yet another bastion of Britishness—serves any interests but those of its members. Here, amid all the appurtenances and amenities of a London gentlemen's club, the old Toronto business elite surveys the rest of the mortal world from a position of fiercely maintained exclusivity.

In times past, British descent was almost essential to reach the top of the economic ladder. From his studies of the Canadian business world, John Porter concluded that well over 80 percent of the nation's economic elite could trace their family origins back to Britain. But the picture has been changing recently, and the Canadian social structure is not nearly as rigid as it was. Fifteen years of government under the French Canadian prime minister, Pierre Trudeau, did much to demolish the traditional pecking order among the nationalities. Other social groups, too, have now achieved at least an equal chance at the top jobs, if not social equality; and there seems to be a consensus developing that Canada will gain if every ethnic group can be seen to have its fair share of the spoils.

The second-largest population grouping, the French Canadians, are concentrated heavily in the province of Quebec and to a lesser extent in New Brunswick. As its people never tire of reminding the rest of Canada and the rest of the world, Quebec is a province "pas comme les autres"—"not like the others." Its distinctiveness results from the stubborn perseverance of the early settlers, for after the final defeat of French Canada in 1763 there was virtually no fresh immigration from

France. Quebec's French identity is still rooted in the French language, which has become more prominent in the province's affairs because of business and immigrant legislation. Linguistic self-determination has gone a long way toward making the Quebecois feel that they are, at long last, "masters in our own house"—the political concept for which the separatists fought during the 1960s and 1970s.

When separatism first became a major issue, the image of the Quebec French was rural and conservative. Their society was dominated on the one hand by tradition and the Catholic church, and on the other by English speakers in Montreal, who controlled most of the province's business institutions. In effect, Montreal, the largest metropolis in all of Canada, was a city where the workers spoke French and the executives spoke English.

Naturally enough, the Quebecois came to feel that they were a conquered people in their own land, and they resented being treated as not quite first-class citizens. But the so-called Quiet Revolution that has been taking place since the 1960s has transformed the situation. The first stirrings presaging that great upheaval can be traced back as far as 1949, when workers at the Johns-Manville Company in the mining town called, from its one resource, Asbestos, went on strike for better pay. The provincial government of the time, led by Maurice Duplessis, brought in the police on the side of the employer; the Catholic church came out on the side of the workers. Many of the politicians who subsequently helped Quebec to pull itself up by its bootstraps first became known at this time—the young Pierre Trudeau was there, marching in sandals and shorts with the

ANATOMY OF A SMALL TOWN

Ever since humorist Stephen Leacock published his *Sunshine Sketches of a Little Town* in 1912 and saw it become a Canadian classic, small-town life has occupied a central place in the nation's self-image. The provincialism and self-importance that Leacock gently mocked seem a small price for the sense of community and relaxed pace of living that he also described.

A writer in search of those positive qualities in the 1980s might have looked in Colborne, Ontario, a modern equivalent of Leacock's fictional town of Mariposa. A close-knit community of 1,800 near the shore of Lake Ontario, it lies just 78 miles east of Toronto, but socially and spiritually it is another world.

Favored with the balmy climate of one of Canada's most temperate regions, Colborne developed as a center of fruit production, especially the growing of apples; local wits christened it "the Little Apple." Even today, a fruit-processing plant is the town's largest employer.

Time has brought other small factories to the town, as well as a clutch of craft and service enterprises, including an artist's studio and a local newspaper, run single-handedly by its editor from home. Colborne no longer boasts, as it did at the turn of the century, an opera house—actually a venue for traveling variety shows. Today, social life centers around the churches—seven in all, each serving separate denominations—and organizations such as the Rotary Club and Women's Institute, which between them run a stream of leisure activities, including beef barbecues, teen dances, and bingo sessions.

Tree-filled gardens surround Colborne's comfortable homes.

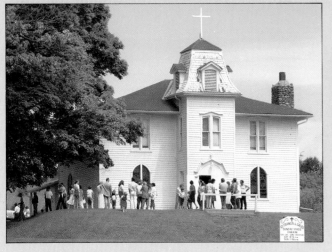

Worshipers head home after Mass at the local Catholic church.

Customers vie for parking spaces opposite the shopping center.

Colborne's part-time firefighters tackle a conflagration.

The editor of the *Colborne Chronicle* works on an article.

Making a home visit, a nurse bandages a patient's arm.

A woodworker turns a dish on a lathe.

strikers—and the left-leaning Liberal party intellectuals who led the Quebecois uprisings in the ensuing years took their cue from the successful outcome of the strike by the laborers at the Johns-Manville Company.

When Duplessis died in 1959, the leader of the opposition Liberal party, Jean Lesage, had a team of eager young men ready to take over the provincial government. An early step was to oversee the nationalization of most of the province's electrical utilities, which were then reorganized under the aegis of Hydro Quebec—now one of the world's biggest public utility companies. More important, in the long run, was Lesage's program of massive investment in education, which broke the church's monopoly on the classroom and also modernized Quebec thinking on social questions and political reform. In effect, it was the Lesage administration that in the end "incorporated Quebec into North America," as one observer described the process, and brought the province linguistic and cultural equality with the English-speaking parts of Canada.

This French-Canadian resurgence turned Montreal into one of the most dynamic cities on the American continent, with beautifully restored historic buildings and a modern center of thriving department stores, banks, and businesses. Momentarily in decline in the early 1970s, it has emerged as a city to which visitors from other provinces, and from the United States, come to enjoy a palpably Gallic atmosphere in an environment where most people understand English. The Montreal of the 1980s is a happy meeting ground of the cultures rather than an arena where the two struggle for supremacy.

One reason for the increased self-confidence of Montreal and of French Canada as a whole is the fact that its inhabitants have drawn closer to their mother country, France. "The airplane and the transistor have done as much as anything to change our perception of ourselves," a businessman explains. "In former days, when ships had to cross the Atlantic and sail upriver 940 miles to reach Montreal, we were a lost colony and our indigenous culture became very provincial. Our language and our customs grew further and further apart from those of France; cultural contact was virtually severed, and from the standpoint of Paris we were an anachronism. But now we see all the latest French movies as soon as they see them in Montparnasse, and our TV screens are filled with everything—good and bad—that French TV and film producers have ever made. We hear the French orchestras, see the French theater companies and ballet troupes, our writers are published in France, our best students go to France—less often to England—to take advanced degrees. Travel is easier, too. Even for the average person, Paris is just around the corner: A round-trip ticket at current rates costs a skilled worker no more than a week's wages. So in the last 30 years, we have grown back together with France. Our roots today are more accessible than they have ever been before."

The French view Quebec more favorably for a number of reasons, not the least of which being the rise of a French-Canadian bureaucracy and the establishment of an entrepreneurial class. Quebec has also become an important partner in France's search for cultural alliances that will help stem the further erosion of French as the language of the world's educated elite. At the university level, scholarship programs and exchange professorships have raised the Quebecois to a position of equality vis-à-vis France, and much of the important research now comes from the Canadian side. It is the University of Montreal Press, for instance, that has undertaken the publication of the prodigious correspondence of France's great 19th-century novelist Emile Zola, with the collaboration of the French National Center for Scientific Research on the project.

Paradoxically, one of the factors that in the past separated the French Canadians from the mother country has been the French language. In their isolation, the Quebecois developed a vocabulary and speech patterns very different from anything to be heard in France itself. In fact, the colloquial French traditionally spoken by rural Quebecois bears about the same relationship to the language of modern France as the English of Appalachian mountain people does to the tongue spoken by the British upper class. Known as *joual*—the word may come from *cheval* (horse) and originally probably meant "the equestrian's language"—it descended from the idiom of the farmers and artisans of Normandy before the language was standardized by the French Academy. The *joual r*, for example, is very much less guttural than the modern Parisian consonant (which is itself, in fact, a relative newcomer to French pronunciation).

In recent years, however, *joual* has been updated and citified to become an urban language that one critic characterizes as "sexy, hip, and very inventive." Understandably, it now contains borrowings and adaptations from the English, such as *le char* for *l'auto* and *la job* in lieu of *le travail*. People say "C'est

3

fun," and garages advertise "Nous fixons les flats." It also includes the only French nonmetric terms of measurement to be found in the world: *pouce* (inch), *pied* (foot), and *verge* (yard) are all used to size up the world in Canada. (Although, ironically, in France itself the last word has entirely different connotations as sexual slang, a fact that sometimes has embarrassing consequences for French Canadians shopping in the mother country.) What is taught in the schools and spoken on TV and radio, however, is standard modern French of the sort that is spoken at the Sorbonne though pronounced with an accent that, to a citizen of France, is instantly recognizable as Canadian.

Whatever form it may take, the French language in Quebec is now on the offensive—a fact quickly brought home to people browsing in Montreal's shopping districts by the French signs that now take precedence over the English. The new dispensation makes it obligatory for shops to display their posters and advertising in French. So department stores with distinctly British names such as Eaton, Simpson, and the Hudson's Bay Company—known here as La Baie—all have busy French copywriting departments. Small shops, too, are expected to comply; a randomly selected issue of the newspaper *La Presse* includes an indignant exposé of the delinquent suburban butcher whose shop-window display had the temerity to proclaim in English: "Special of the Week—Boneless Pork Roast." The transgression of this hapless shopkeeper rated a front-page photo in the second section of the paper under the accusatory headline "Small Businesses Multiply the Offenses."

On the streets, however, English has disappeared completely. Injunctions

that were bilingual at one time—for example, the formerly ubiquitous Stop-Arret signs (which the city's Jewish population cheerfully distorted into "Stop, already")—now come in only one version: French. The underlying anxiety reflected in this kind of linguistic discrimination is that if English is not prevented from infiltrating the Francophone cities, all French culture will ultimately disappear from North America. Similarly, the French Canadians are worried by their falling birthrate, which suggests that their culture may finally be swallowed up in a sea of Anglophones. In times past, French Canadians were always able to fall back on their expanding population—the so-called revenge of the cradle—as a means of stemming the English-speaking tide. Now, the falling demographic curve gives even the most liberal of French-Canadian leaders cause for concern.

Separatism, then, still has a constituency. Indeed, many of the province's best artists and intellectuals have long been identified with the Parti Québécois. When writer Fernand Dumont won the coveted Governor-General's Prize of the Arts Council of Canada, he went to Ottawa to collect the prize and then, in a much-publicized gesture, donated the money to the very party that was threatening to secede from Ottawa and break up the Arts Council. The irony of this was not lost on some indignant Ontarians, but Dumont's peer group, the Anglophone writers, proved to be so disarmingly sympathetic that they in fact took the wind out of Dumont's sails.

The poet Al Purdy neatly summed up the Anglo-intellectuals' attitude in a long poem entitled "A Handful of Earth," which he dedicated to the sep-

aratist Quebec premier and founder of the Parti Québécois, Réné Lévesque:

Proposal:
let us join Quebec
if Quebec won't join us
I don't mind in the least
being governed from Quebec City
by Canadiens instead of Canadians
in fact the fleur-de-lis and maple leaf
in my bilingual guts
bloom incestuous . . .

It is not easy to work up any lasting indignation against such conciliatory compatriots, however passionate the cause. Hence tempers have cooled, and French Canadians as a whole have evidently decided that it is better to be a privileged province within a great nation than a rump state in a fragmented Canada—which in the future might run the risk of being swallowed up by the United States.

Numerically, Canadians from other non-British backgrounds loom as large in the population as French Canadians. Yet their influence on the country is far less significant, since the diversity of their origins prevents them from speaking with a concerted voice. Most of these groups have gradually assimilated with the English speakers as a way of easing their passage into Canadian society. The process of adjustment is fraught with pitfalls—and has produced some of the best and funniest of Canadian writing, by chroniclers eager to record this rite of passage in all its rich, astonishing detail. Toronto's 400,000 Italian Canadians, for example, have made the transition to English by means of an intriguing halfway language that tries to encompass the best of both worlds. As Norman Hartley re-

Braced against the wind, a woman crosses Portage Bridge, which spans the Ottawa River to link Ottawa with the city of Hull, Quebec. The federal capital is usually under snow for four to five months a year; isolated drifts, their melting slowed by debris inside them, may last until summer.

ported in the *Globe and Mail,* these Italian Canadians start the day with "a brecchifesti of becon or amma with a slice of ciso," and then in the evening, when they go to a drive-in movie, they discuss whether "to put grevi or chicciappa (ketchup) on their frencifrai—always assuming, of course, that they don't order a bag of pappacorna or pinozze (peanuts)."

It is by such small steps that foreigners are absorbed into the mainstream of Canadian culture. In the words of pioneer socialist leader J. S. Woodsworth, their presence compels the old-established Canadians to "make deeper and broader the foundations of our national life."

The list of minority groups who have undergone this transition is a long and remarkable one. Some have come from countries such as Norway and Sweden, whose inhabitants were already accustomed to a life of toil in near-arctic weather conditions and who knew how to make the most of the rich and extensive natural resources that Canada offers loggers, miners, and fishermen who are able to cope with the intemperate climate.

Finnish immigration, though it represents only a fraction of 1 percent of Canada's population, does provide a notable case of a people who saw the vast northern wilderness as a land full of opportunity. Finland, the most

A METROPOLIS RIDING HIGH ON OIL

Ranch horses gallop across a bare Alberta hillside, against a backdrop of the modern skyline of Calgary rising from the plain.

northerly country in the world after Iceland, sent more than 80,000 settlers, many of whom went to work in the industries they knew best—lumbering and mining—in northern Ontario and in British Columbia. Others, equally undeterred by cold and rugged frontier conditions, carved homesteads out of the forest wilderness in communities such as Timmins, South Porcupine, and Cochrane, Ontario, building log cabins and a sauna and felling trees to sell to the local lumber mills. The descendants of these hardy pioneers still celebrate the midsummer festival in Finnish national costume, singing the old songs around a bonfire. But in most respects, the Finnish Canadians—once noted for their utopian and radical ideas—have blended quietly into their local communities. A blue-and-white Finnish flag as a bumper sticker is often their only distinguishing mark.

German Canadians make up the nation's third-largest ethnic group, and economically they have long been counted among its most successful.

Oil-company airplanes fill a hangar at the Executive Flight Center.

Cowboy boots gleam on display racks in a downtown shoe store.

No Canadian city has seen such a rapid and total transformation in recent years as Calgary. Originally a North West Mounted Police post established in the wilderness in 1875, it was developed by the firm building the Canadian Pacific Railway, which reached it in 1883. It first won prosperity as a railhead for Alberta's cattle ranchers. Soon it was a railhead for wheat, and its fortunes rose with the grain boom.

Another economic resource brought the great changes of the postwar years. As the seat of Alberta's first refinery in 1923, the city was well placed to take advantage of the bonanza that followed the opening of the province's major oil fields after 1947. When world oil prices quadrupled following the OPEC crisis of 1974, Calgary became Canada's most spectacular boom town. Skyscrapers sprouted in the old town center, and the population increased by 50 percent within the decade.

Although the mid-1980s downturn in oil prices shook the city, Calgary retains its faith in the future. At the same time, it takes pride in its cowtown origins, celebrated annually in the bronco-busting and chuckwagon-racing of the Calgary Stampede.

Many recent German immigrants have quickly become prosperous, thanks to the skills and assets they brought with them from Europe. "I was raised on a large family farm in the Rhine valley," explains a determined woman in her seventies, now the owner of a large cattle ranch in British Columbia. "During World War II, I was a German army nurse; but at the war's end, I found myself working as an interpreter in a Canadian army field hospital. I liked these people so well I decided to emigrate to Canada as soon as I could. When my father died, I sold my share of the family estate to my brothers and took the money to Canada, where I invested it in a small farm and enough livestock to start a herd. Later I moved to a new site, bought 10 times as much land, and employed local Indians as ranch hands. It all worked out beyond my wildest expectations: I've had the time of my life and now specialize in breeding saddle horses. God and Canada have been very good to me!"

German settlers had been actively re-

Cruise boats used for trips along the
St. Lawrence River lie berthed in
Montreal's Old Town, near the
church of Notre Dame de Bonsecours.
The city, with its stylish boutiques
and animated nightlife, is one of
Canada's major tourist attractions,
drawing 1.5 million visitors in 1984.

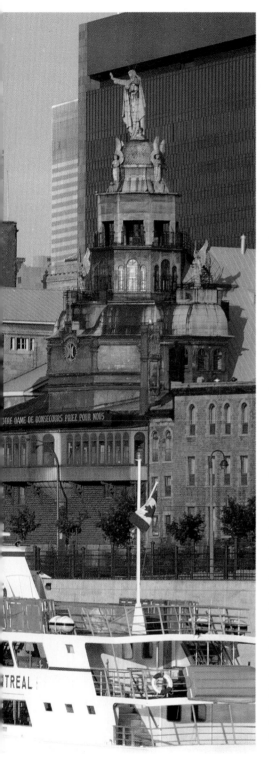

cruited by the British colonial government as early as 1750; a century later, there were more than 150,000 Germans in Ontario, the vanguard of more than one million who eventually migrated to Canada. Many of them settled in the fertile agricultural region surrounding "Canada's German Capital," an Ontario town they had renamed Berlin. There the Union Jack and the German flag flew side by side, and both Queen Victoria's and the kaiser's birthdays were celebrated as civic holidays. Later waves of immigration brought a massive influx of Germans to the Prairie Provinces, and the towns of Winnipeg, Regina, and Calgary all acquired sizable Germantowns.

The outbreak of World War I placed these immigrants and their offspring in a cruel dilemma. Germany had now become the enemy and an object of universal condemnation; as loyal Canadians, they felt obliged to dissociate themselves from everything German. Berlin, Ontario, was renamed Kitchener in honor of Britain's famous general; in western Canada, names such as Bremen, Koblenz, and Kaiser disappeared from the map. German-language newspapers were suppressed, churches ceased holding services in German, and German schools were closed. When immigration from Germany resumed after the war, the new settlers carefully refrained from displays of German patriotism and made haste to become Canadian citizens. At the outbreak of World War II, only 16,000 German Canadians had not already become citizens. No more than a handful were interned as "enemy aliens," moreover, for the government could detect no pro-Nazi sympathies even among that small minority.

The aftermath of the war displaced millions of ethnic Germans from their homes in such countries as Poland, Russia, Rumania, and Czechoslovakia, and brought many East Germans to the West as homeless refugees. About 300,000 of these immigrants came to Canada during the 1950s and 1960s. Many were farmers, accompanied by their families, who settled in western Canada, attracted by the availability of fertile farmland. Gradually, however, even these tenacious farmers have followed the general movement off the land and into the towns and cities, so that the great majority of them now live in urban centers.

Only the German-descended Mennonites and Hutterites have, for religious reasons, held themselves apart from the "temptations" and "rewards" of modern life. Throughout Canada there are almost 1,000 Mennonite Christian congregations, whose 190,000 members carry on the austere pietist traditions espoused by the 15th-century Dutch Protestant leader Menno Simons. The Mennonites took their ideas from the Anabaptists, who opposed infant baptism and advocated instead "true baptism" for adults on the basis of voluntary faith. Every Mennonite believer was himself a "priest," carrying the spirit of God—an extraordinary concept in a feudal age, and so dangerously egalitarian as to provoke the authorities into a century of violent repression and persecution. Yet somehow the Mennonites survived torture and mass execution and were able to establish close-knit communal fellowships in Holland, England, and Switzerland as well as in Germany.

They first came to North America in the 1680s to found communities in Pennsylvania. Among those who have since settled in Canada, the Old Order

3

Residents of Westmount, a wealthy enclave favored by Montreal's English-speaking minority, enjoy a sedate game of bowls. The sport was popularized in Canada mainly by emigrants from Scotland, where its code of play was drawn up in 1849.

Mennonites, who are in the minority, still make no concessions at all to the 20th century and decline to use such conveniences as the telephone and the automobile. They have retained an 18th-century rural life-style along with the German language and liturgy; and their clothing styles have not changed for more than 150 years. The continuation of the Old Order requires that the Mennonites refrain from sending their children to state-run schools and prevents them from obtaining a university education, though the ones most gifted in book-learning are sent to special seminaries. The more flexible majority, known as Conference Mennonites, now vote in state and local elections, and a number have served in municipal, provincial, and federal offices. Nearly 50 percent of Mennonite marriages in the 1980s, moreover, are to

men or women of other denominations. The Mennonites have also proselytized successfully beyond their own ranks, so that Canadian-Mennonite communities now include people of French, Chinese, Indian, and Anglo-Saxon extraction.

In many parts of western Canada, Polish, Ukrainian, and Russian immigrants have played an important part in the establishment of farms and agricultural settlements. At first, they frequently had language problems and were resented by their Anglophone neighbors. In one Saskatchewan town mentioned in Barry Broadfoot's oral history of Canada, *Ten Lost Years,* a Polish-born doctor and his family were gradually joined by half a dozen of their relatives, who bought local farms and also set up a grain and feed store on Main Street. The doctor's son remem-

bered feeling very much at home in that "good place" until he overheard the town's banker telling a friend: "Looks like the miserable hunkies are taking over this whole town." The doctor was shocked when he heard about it, but he controlled his temper and told his son: "I guess that proves we'll just have to be twice as good citizens as anybody else."

Some of the Slavic immigrants with strong religious convictions saw no reason to change their ways in order to conform to the prevailing Anglo-Saxon patterns of behavior. The Russian sect known as Doukhobors—"Spirit Wrestlers"—were militantly nonconformist under the tsarist regime and remained stubborn dissenters when they settled in Saskatchewan and British Columbia. They clung firmly to their social and religious customs, which sprang from the belief that God dwells in each man and woman and not in a church.

Accordingly, most of the 15,000 practicing Doukhobors are pacifists, rejecting the authority of both church liturgy and the secular state. They live in austere Russian-speaking communities where borscht, kasha—buckwheat groats—and the fermented drink kvass form an important part of their vegetarian diet. The Doukhobors have now split into several branches: Members of one of the fiercer groups have been known to stage nude protest parades and to burn their own schools and barns to underscore their contempt for material possessions. Their children, however, are drifting away to join the society of "uptown Canada" in ever-increasing numbers.

The immigrants who came from the world's warmer climates have usually had to make even more difficult adjustments to Canadian reality. Indeed, after the first few thousand immigrants from India had aroused the racial fears of the Vancouver authorities, any further influxes of newcomers from the subcontinent were excluded on the pretext that climate and culture made these immigrants unfit for work in Canada—and thus likely to become public charges. In fact, the Sikhs from the Punjab who came to western Canada early in the century were hardy, skilled workers who gravitated to the lumber industry where they specialized in handling logs in the sawmills of Victoria, Vancouver, and New Westminster. It was not until 1947 that people from the Indian subcontinent received the right to vote in British Columbia: Four years later, government regulations finally permitted the entry of fresh immigrants from India, Pakistan, and Sri Lanka.

By 1980, the number of Canadians whose ancestors originated on the Indian subcontinent came to more than 160,000. Many of them had arrived from places such as East Africa, Mauritius, and Fiji, where there were large Indian colonies. One group of 25,000 English-speaking Ismailis—a progressive Muslim sect that had originated in India but settled in Kenya and Uganda—came to Canada to escape Idi Amin's anti-Asian persecutions. Another smaller group of French-

A customer at a café in Montreal's Rue Crescent pours a drink for his companion. The echoes of France in the city's street life recall its claim to be, after Paris, the largest French-language community: 1.7 million of its 2.8 million inhabitants speak French as their mother tongue.

In a home in Saskatchewan, women prepare scores of piroshki, a Ukrainian speciality of pastry stuffed with a meat-and-vegetable filling. More than half a million people of Ukrainian origin live in Canada, most of them in the Prairie Provinces or in Ontario.

speaking Ismailis from Zaire, the Ivory Coast, and Madagascar settled in the Montreal area.

Most of the Ugandan refugees, Hindu as well as Ismaili, knew nothing at all about Canada when they filled in their applications for immigration visas. For them, the nation was simply a refuge of last resort in a world that on every other side had closed its doors to them. One skilled Gujarati watchmaker, who now owns several Canadian watch and camera shops, recalls that his immigration in 1970 was a "traumatic experience." He and his father had been stripped of all their belongings back in Kampala,

and they arrived penniless aboard a government-chartered plane full of refugees. "We didn't know what we were going to do when we arrived, where we would live, and what to expect"; but a reception center had been prepared for them in an unused army barracks, and "we were amazed to find that the Canadian people and their government were so kind. A man said 'Bienvenue' to all of us. 'Relax,' he said. 'Relax tonight and we will talk about everything in the morning.'"

The next day, they were housed in a Montreal hotel and were given warm clothing. He and his father found jobs

almost immediately in the watch-repair department of the city's leading jewelry shop; to get them started, a tool company let them have more than $500 worth of tools on credit. After living in the rapacious world of Idi Amin, the son said, "We just couldn't believe it was possible."

The rest of his tale follows the familiar upward curve of the Horatio Alger-style success story, with hard work duly rewarded by prosperity. In five years, he and his father had opened their first shop; to make certain it was run according to the latest principles, the son took university courses in computer technology, management science, human relations, and psychology. He and his wife—a Ugandan Indian who is now a senior officer in a bank—bought a house and a car, traveled to Europe and Florida, and remain fervently loyal Canadians. "Multiculturalism really does work in Montreal and I have always been well treated," he concludes.

Not all immigrants are as warmly received as the watchmaker, and indeed the friendly reception granted to him would be resented by some Canadians as preferential treatment. Nonetheless, there are hundreds of such stories among the East Asian immigrants, who have become an important factor in the Canadian retail trade, launching new shops and enterprises in cities such as Vancouver, Calgary, and Edmonton. They include many Sunni Muslims from Pakistan. A high proportion of professionals such as teachers, university professors, and doctors number among their ranks. Among them, the process of assimilation has proceeded more rapidly than with earlier groups. Although many have brought wives from Pakistan and raised their families in the traditional Muslim way, there is a growing tendency to Canadianize; about 20 percent of this more recently arrived educated elite have Canadian, British, or American wives.

The 300,000 Chinese in Canada, living mainly in the Chinatowns of Toronto and Vancouver, have had to contend with many of the same problems that the Indians and Pakistanis face. During the 1880s, more than 15,000 Chinese laborers were brought in to build the Canadian Pacific Railway. Others did much of the hewing of wood and carrying of water in the sawmills, canneries, and market gardens of the pioneer industrial economy. Yet, in 1902, Chinese and Japanese immigrants were declared unfit for full citizenship and dangerous to the state. Restrictions on their immigration were not entirely lifted until the 1960s—by which time the resident community had elected the first Chinese-Canadian member of Parliament.

Almost all of the earliest Chinese immigrants came from villages in the Pearl River Delta, between Canton and Hong Kong. Since 1950, however, most have come from Hong Kong. They often speak English fluently and belong to a highly skilled, well-educated professional and technical elite. Recently, the Canadian government has been actively recruiting the city-state's entrepreneurs in the hope that they will bring their talents—and also their assets—to Canada before Hong Kong rejoins mainland China in 1997.

The Japanese Canadians have had a less happy history. In the wake of the bombing of the U.S. Navy at Pearl Harbor in 1941, they became the object of bitter official hostility. The federal government invoked the War Measures Act to remove forcibly all citizens of Japanese extraction from an area within 100 miles of the Pacific, on the grounds that they posed a threat to national security. About 20,000 people were evacuated to hastily built camps, and their homes, businesses, and property were sold for a fraction of their real value—a grievance that remained a live political issue in Canada into the 1980s. Now, however, a substantial community is back on the West Coast, working as fishermen, as free-lance gardeners, in restaurants, and in the professions; and western Canada is now a magnet for Japanese tourists.

Ironically, the only groups who have been consistently shortchanged in the

Mennonite youngsters wearing the plain dress of their community play in a field near Elmira, Ontario. Members of a strict Protestant sect, Mennonites are often hostile to public education. Today, 14 percent of their children go to private schools—more than twice the national average.

AN ANCIENT PEOPLE FACING NEW WAYS

Residents of Paulatuk on the northern edge of the Northwest Territories arrive by snowmobile for a church service.

Watched by hunting companions, an Inuit man *(above)* leans over a pond to float eider-duck eggs taken from a nearby nest. If the eggs do not sink, they are infertile and may be eaten.

A dog team pulls a hunter across an icy waste. Though snowmobiles are now widely used, sleds are still popular, as dogs are cheap to feed and more reliable than machines.

Life for the 27,000 Inuit of the Northwest Territories has changed irrevocably in recent decades. With the exploitation of the Far North's mineral resources, the Inuit have been increasingly exposed to modern ways. Few follow their ancestors' semi-nomadic life-style. Instead, most live in settlements of prefabricated frame houses provided by the government across the territory.

Materially, they are better off than ever before. Starvation is no longer a danger. Many own television sets and snowmobiles; all benefit from health care and free schooling. But alcoholism has become a problem, and many individuals have had difficulty in adjusting to the rigid schedules of salaried jobs.

Nevertheless, the modern world has not eradicated Inuit pride. Many men still hunt caribou and seal at least part time and continue using their inherited skills of wilderness survival.

Fishing through an ice hole near Paulatuk, an Inuit lands a catch of arctic char.

process of developing are the Indians and Inuit, who were in Canada before the immigrants and who lived on the land as hunter-gatherers but did not farm it. As an Indian chief named Dan George neatly summed up the matter: "When the white man came, we had the land and they had the Bibles; now they have the land and we have the Bibles." In the late 1980s, there were more Indians, not fewer, than when the first European settlers learned from them how to survive in the forests of the New World. Their registered population in 1980 was 316,737—but this figure takes into account only those who still chose to be counted as Indians; many more of them have been quietly absorbed into modern urban Canada without leaving a trace of their origins in the census figures.

Under the Indian Act of 1951, the "registered Indians" have title to more than 2,200 reservations, only 800 of which are actually inhabited; about one third of the Indian population lives permanently outside the reservations. Few still practice their traditional subsistence economy, though in the north a considerable number live by fishing, trapping, and hunting. A majority of those in employment, however, are now wage earners, working as farmhands, loggers, or laborers. A fortunate few have managed to earn a modern living by practicing their traditional arts and crafts. One of the two great moccasin-making establishments in Canada, for example, is a Huron Indian crafts center in the province of Quebec. But far too often, the adjustment to the modern world has meant that Indians have had to give up their traditional skills and a way of life that was perfectly suited to the land in exchange for what is a distinctly second-rate

version of white society's life-style.

The Indians of the Pacific Coast, for example, possessed one of the world's most artistically fertile cultures when explorers such as Captain Cook first encountered them. "Everything they have," Cook wrote in 1778, "is as well and ingeniously made, as if they were furnished with the most complete tool chest. Their invention and dexterity, in all manual works, is at least equal to that of any other nation."

But their 2,000-year-old culture was soon destroyed by contact with the Europeans' version of civilization. The Nootka, Kwakiutl, and Haida tribes gave up their great houses, with their stately complement of totem poles, and moved into clapboard houses; they traded their 130-foot-long canoes, in which they hunted whales in the open Pacific, for modern fishing boats with outboard engines. The famous West Coast potlatches, the marathon ceremonial feasts at which a host would attempt to overwhelm his guests with the sheer scope of his gift giving, were formally prohibited by an uncomprehending Canadian government that wanted to prevent these "wasteful" Indians from foolishly impoverishing themselves by this custom.

In one famous incident at Alert Bay, in 1921, the Kwakiutl chief Daniel Cranmer (known among his own people as Gwagwadaxala) was arrested with 50 of his guests after giving a princely potlatch. The local Indian agent confiscated three boatloads of precious ceremonial sculptures, most notably masks and rattles, which were then sold at ludicrous prices to museums in Toronto, Ottawa, and New York. When the Indians sent an emissary to Ottawa 30 years later to offer to buy the treasures back, the National

3

Museum flatly refused their request. But the director who took over the museum in 1967 had more modern ideas and offered to return the confiscated potlatch collection, provided that the Indians would build an appropriate museum in which to house it. The villages to which the objects belonged eventually built two small but superb museums in which to display their ancestral sculptures—museums symbolizing the revival of Indian culture along the coast of British Columbia.

The inauguration of the U'mista Museum at Alert Bay in 1980—the name means "a safe homecoming for someone who has been held captive abroad"—was attended not only by the regional chiefs in ceremonial robes and button blankets, but by government dignitaries, church officials, museum curators, anthropologists, and a scattering of international art collectors. The event was celebrated with dances that were filmed by camera crews from the Canadian Broadcasting Corporation; art experts in the audience pointed out that some of the Indian dance masks and rattles that had been sold for a few dollars 60 years before would now fetch anywhere between $50,000 and $150,000 apiece at auction.

But most Indians derive little practical benefit from this upsurge of interest in the art of their grandfathers. Unemployment levels among the Indians are twice as high as the national average; and by most other sociological measures, their economy compares poorly with that of other Canadians. Poor living standards on the reservations are caused partly by the remoteness of these areas: Nearly half of them are inaccessible by road. The prospects of Indians who leave for the cities, however, are not a great deal brighter. Unable to adjust to urban life, many turn to drink, which is blamed for a crime rate among Indians that is three to five times higher than the average for the nation as a whole.

Georges Erasmus, the president of Canada's largest aboriginal organization, the Assembly of First Nations, has referred to his people, the Dene, as "the colony within." The major issue facing them and other Indian groups is the clash between their culture and the demands of an advancing industrial technology. When the Europeans arrived in Canada, he writes, "we were treated as incompetent to make decisions for ourselves. Europeans would treat us in such a way as to make us feel that they knew, better than we ourselves, what was good for us."

Thanks to organizations such as the Assembly of First Nations, however, peoples like the Dene have acquired a great deal of political influence during the past 20 years. In 1969, they conducted a successful fight to defeat an attempt to repeal the Indian Act, which would have left a great many of them defenseless in their dealings with the government and with the powerful oil, lumber, and mining companies.

The Inuit never came under the provisions of the Indian Act, but they too are increasingly active in political matters. There are about 27,000 of them, divided among eight groups, but all speak the same language. Living in the Far North, they were long isolated from the rest of Canada by geography; but since World War II, the rapid development of air travel and the building of defense installations and meteorological and communications stations have effectively ended this isolation. Few Inuit now follow their traditional way of life. Most are Christian; increasingly, igloos have been replaced by cabins, kayaks by motorized canoes, and dogsleds by snowmobiles. Yet hunting remains their main occupation, and the old, functional dress of sealskin boots and caribou parkas is still retained. A growing awareness of the need to protect their heritage and identity led to the foundation of the Inuit Brotherhood in 1971, while Inuit cooperatives, which were initiated by the federal government in 1959, now do more than $30 million (Canadian) worth of business every year.

Clearly there are strains and stresses in the political fabric that will exercise the nation's best minds for years to come, but the government does what it can to help every identifiable ethnic group find its place in the sun. The Canadian Broadcasting Company, for example, has launched a special training program in broadcast journalism for members of minority groups. The Canadian Film Board has undertaken to expand its aid to filmmakers trying to produce material in what it describes as "their ancestral languages." The country's libraries benefit from a Multilingual Biblioservice that provides books in the eight minority languages most in demand as well as material in other languages on request: The goal is to cover the majority of languages spoken in Canada.

The National Library and the Public Archives in Ottawa have instituted a special program for minorities; there is a Canadian Center for Folk Culture Studies at the National Museum of Man; special efforts are made by federal ministries to accommodate the needs of peoples of all the races and nationalities embraced in the Canadian mosaic. Cynics say that these efforts are partly a political ploy designed for the

purpose of winning votes. But while there may indeed be a pork-barrel aspect to Canada's ethnic programs, altruistic motives are also at work. Canada is the product of so many different ethnic strains that it is impossible for Canadians to take a strong or proselytizing attitude toward their national identity, and multiculturalism is the only possible policy that can override the divisions of such a fragmented pluralist society.

In the last analysis, Canada manages to hang together as a nation in spite of all this diversity. A number of subtle factors are responsible for the tacit understanding held by all the groups and subgroups that they will support the democratic political process and subscribe to the shared ideal of live and let live. One factor is a shared belief in liberal social values. Increasingly, fear of coming under U.S. domination has also helped give Canadians a common

sense of identity. But there is also a conviction in the inherent rightness of the Canadian way of life, a belief that the Canadian experience has shown that multiplicity is superior to uniformity. In the words of a former minister responsible for multiculturalism: "Much of the richness and vitality of our economic and social life is due to the energy of the many different cultural and racial groups that have made Canada their home." □

Geometrically functional buildings dwarf a turn-of-the-century commercial structure in Toronto's business center. The city is Canada's financial capital, boasting one of North America's leading stock exchanges as well as the headquarters of major banks and investment companies.

102

THE SOURCES OF POWER

A Canadian reality about power is that not all that much of it actually resides in Canada. The limits of power are, of course, a fact of life for all nation-states in today's interdependent "global village"—itself a term coined by a Canadian, the communications guru Marshall McLuhan. Canada, being a country of 25 million people next door to a superpower, feels this truth more than most. Yet some observers insist that if the nation is judged in terms of its economic performance, it stands not simply as a middle power such as Australia or Sweden but actually as a major, or principal, force of the rank of the United Kingdom, France, or West Germany. Evidence to support this view accrued in 1986, when Canada became a full participating member in the annual meetings of the so-called Group of Seven industrialized nations, along with the United Kingdom, France, and West Germany, plus Japan, Italy, and of course, the United States.

In any event, it is the Canadian practice to take what power there is and spread it thin. The hallmark of the Canadian political system is its federalism and the remarkable extent to which power is passed down to the level of the 10 provinces. (It has been jokingly said that when a Canadian student is asked to write an essay on just about any topic, that student's first impulse is to put as the subtitle: "Is It a Federal or Provincial Responsibility?") This decentralization is a response to both the vastness of the country and to the insistence of French-speaking Quebecois on strong provincial rights that serve to protect their language and culture: Therefore, all the other provinces received these powers, too.

The media have made people only too well aware of the comings and goings of those visible purveyors of power, the politicians. In Canada, the politicians wheel and deal within a parliamentary system. When Canadians speak of Parliament, they are usually referring to simply the House of Commons—and, indeed, that is where the action is—but strictly speaking, the Parliament also includes a second, upper chamber, the Senate, and the governor-general, who acts as the representative of the British monarch, Canada's nominal head of state.

The House of Commons consists of 282 members of Parliament (MPs), most of whom represent the two main political parties, the Liberals and the Conservatives. Though voted out of office in 1984, the Liberals have historically dominated federal politics to the point that they have been called "the government party." Liberal success has been a tribute to the party's ability to win majorities in both English-speaking Canada and French-speaking Quebec and to sprawl across the political center, albeit with a slight reformist tilt to the left. Since confederation in 1867, only one Liberal leader (Edward Blake in the 1880s) has failed to become prime minister. The quintessential Liberal, Mackenzie King, remained in power for a total of almost 22 years between 1921 and 1948. He thereby outperformed his leading Conservative rival, Canada's first prime minister, Sir John A. Macdonald, who lasted for 19 years, being in office from 1867 until his death in 1891, with a five-year interval in the 1870s.

The tendency thereafter of the Conservatives to languish in opposition reflects the party's inability to win a majority in Quebec. However, there have been two striking exceptions to this trend following the landslide victories of John Diefenbaker in 1958 and Brian Mulroney in 1984. Philosophically, the Conservatives have also been largely of the centrist persuasion. Although the proper name of the party since 1942 has been the Progressive Conservatives, and though it has its reformers (sometimes characterized by the oxymoron Red Tories), it has veered to the right in recent neoconservative times when it moves off dead center.

The longest-running smaller party, with a federal presence since the 1940s, is the left-of-center New Democratic party: A minority grouping in English-speaking Canada, it is virtually nonexistent in Quebec. From a European perspective—where social democracy is part of the political landscape—what is striking is the party's weakness. But from a North American perspective, its very existence is noteworthy; while the United States has an organized socialist party, its following and voting power are very small.

Canada's government of the day must have the support of a majority of MPs, either from its own party or, if it is a minority government, with the help of votes from other, smaller groupings. In 6 of the 11 elections from 1957 to

4

1984, no party did win a majority, and three times in that period, elections were brought on by defeats of minority governments in the Commons. The leader of the majority, or dominant, party becomes the prime minister; he (it has yet to be otherwise in Canada, although the first female governor-general was named in 1984) chooses ministers to head government departments, such as finance and justice, from among the leading members of his party. Together they make up the cabinet, which exercises the executive power of the government. In forming his cabinet, the prime minister must also take into account provincial representation. If the governing party has little or no representation from a region of importance in the House of Commons, which has been the case on several occasions for the Conservatives in Quebec and the Liberals in the west, the prime minister can look to the upper house, and a senator from the appropriate area may be chosen.

On the walls of the Senate hangs a quotation from Cicero: "It is the duty of the nobles to oppose the fickleness of the multitude." As conceived in 1867, the upper house was supposed to protect regional interests, with smaller provinces being guaranteed a minimum number of seats, and it is still intended to perform that function today. Its members are not elected, however; instead, they are appointed by the government of the day, as seats fall vacant. The senators remain there until they reach the age of 75. By the 1980s, its anomalous nonelective nature and the frequency of nominations based on little more than loyalty to the reigning party have left the Senate with slight legitimacy in the eyes of the public. In theory, the Senate is very powerful and able to veto legislation passed by the House of Commons; but in fact, it does little and would seem ripe for abolition. Thoughtful political scientists, however, have been more inclined to advocate that the Senate be reformed as an elected body that can properly represent and protect the regions within the national government.

Like other countries in the Commonwealth, Canada is a constitutional monarchy, and since the earliest days of its colonial history, a governor or governor-general, serving as the representative of the Crown, has been the acting head of state. By the mid-1980s, the position had only symbolic import; the prime minister is the real leader. He appoints the governor-general by nominating the candidate of his choice to the sovereign. As a stand-in for the reigning British monarch, however, the governor-general does serve the useful function of lessening ceremonial demands on the prime minister. The first Canadian prime minister was appointed in 1952; appointments since then have alternated between a Francophone and an Anglophone, although being bilingual is nowadays a prerequisite for either.

The British tie—of which the office of governor-general is a surviving symbol—now has decreasing meaning even to English-speaking Canadians, more and more of whom trace their ancestry not to Great Britain but to a multitude of other countries. The Commonwealth lingers on, but it is now the American connection that matters overwhelmingly to Canada's economy and culture.

Still, the influence of the Crown has been a shaping force in the country's history. The Canadian tendency to defer to the government—to give author-

SHARED DECISION MAKING IN A FEDERAL STATE

Canada is a federation of 10 provinces and two territories in which much power is devolved from the state. Although the legitimate limits of its mandate are not always clear-cut, the federal government, based in Ottawa, deals with matters of national interest, including defense and foreign affairs. The governments of the 10 provinces supervise education, natural resources, health, and social services. The Yukon and Northwest territories, with their scattered populations, are governed by the federal authorities, who appoint commissioners to consult with locally elected bodies.

The structures of the federal and provincial systems are alike: The head of state is the Crown's representative—federally, the governor-general and provincially, the lieutenant-governors. But these officers are appointed on the recommendations of the federal prime minister. The prime minister—always the leader of the largest party in the House of Commons—names the cabinet and nominates candidates for the nonelective Senate, whose function is to simplify and tidy legislation passed by the elected members of the Commons.

YUKON TERRITORY   NORTHWEST TERRITORIES

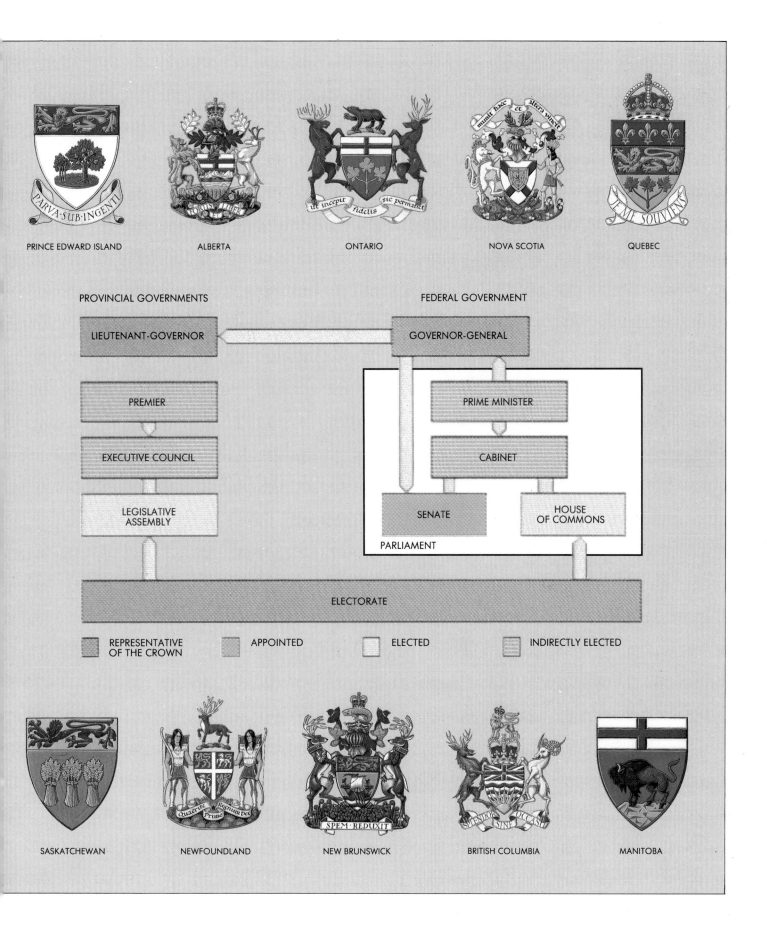

PRINCE EDWARD ISLAND   ALBERTA   ONTARIO   NOVA SCOTIA   QUEBEC

PROVINCIAL GOVERNMENTS   FEDERAL GOVERNMENT

LIEUTENANT-GOVERNOR   GOVERNOR-GENERAL

PREMIER

PRIME MINISTER

EXECUTIVE COUNCIL

CABINET

LEGISLATIVE ASSEMBLY

SENATE   HOUSE OF COMMONS

PARLIAMENT

ELECTORATE

REPRESENTATIVE OF THE CROWN   APPOINTED   ELECTED   INDIRECTLY ELECTED

SASKATCHEWAN   NEWFOUNDLAND   NEW BRUNSWICK   BRITISH COLUMBIA   MANITOBA

Cadets of the Royal Military College in Kingston, Ontario, stand to attention at a parade. The oldest of Canada's military training institutions, the college prepares its students for careers as officers in the nation's 50,000-strong regular army.

ity the benefit of the doubt; not to question the federal government the way, for example, Americans do—is in part a consequence of that monarchical tradition, which was never overthrown by a war of independence. It was not until 1965 that Canada got its own flag. The patriation of the Constitution in 1982 finally ended the anachronism that required Canada to resort to the British Parliament for amendments, but cabinet ministers are still called Ministers of the Crown, and publicly owned companies, both federal and provincial, are Crown corporations.

In practice, though, the Crown entrusts all its powers to the governor-general. The queen and members of the royal family are always made welcome on their visits to Canada; of course, the Americans now welcome them freely as well.

Each of the 10 provinces operates politically under a single-chamber parliamentary structure. Each has its own premier—the provincial equivalent of the prime minister—and a cabinet that exercises executive power. But the Crown is present, in the form of a federally appointed lieutenant-governor who is responsible for supervising the affairs of the province. As in the case of the governor-general, the lieutenant-governor's duties are purely ceremonial. Canadian novelist Robertson Davies's Deptford trilogy revolves around the mysterious death of sugar magnate Boy Staunton, who apparently took his own life a few days before he was to have been appointed the lieutenant-governor of Ontario; he had been dismayed, we are told, when he realized the schedule of ceremonial functions—"a tyranny of duty"—he must assume.

While only two parties, the Liberals and the Conservatives, have been able to win the votes necessary to govern nationally, at the provincial level there has been more ideological diversity. Recent years have seen the left-of-center New Democratic party and the right-of-center Social Credit form governments in the western provinces, as well as the separatist and social democratic Parti Québécois in Quebec. Canadians also like, in an evenhanded way, to vote for one party nationally and another provincially. After the Conservatives defeated the Liberals nationally in 1984, the 42-year-old Conservative government in Ontario was finally replaced by the Liberals in the following year. This propensity to countervail might be thought by some to have bordered on the schizophrenic when, in elections in the 1970s, Quebecois voted for the federalist Trudeau nationally and for the separatist Lévesque in their own province.

The fathers of confederation, being centralists at heart, allotted the most important powers to the new federal government. Included in this category were those powers that were thought to be necessary for nation building and for economic development: money and banking, trade and transportation, as well as criminal law, Indian affairs, defense, and external affairs. (However, external affairs was not fully separated from Westminster until 1931.) To the provinces went "generally all matters of a merely local or private nature": education, civil law (including property and civil rights), health and welfare, natural resources, and local government. The federal and provincial governments were both granted concurrent powers with respect to immigration and agriculture. And because the federal government received the most important responsibilities, so too

RESORTS IN THE ROCKIES

CANADIAN PACIFIC

A cover illustration for a 1930s travel brochure uses the image of a smartly turned-out Mountie to promote the Canadian Pacific Railway and the Banff Springs Hotel. Set up in 1873, the Mounted Police long ago attained the status of a national symbol.

Attempting to douse a forest fire, a CL-215 jettisons its load of nearly 1,585 U.S. gallons of water in less than one second. Overseas customers buy many of these aircraft, which can fill their tanks in under 10 seconds by skimming over lake surfaces.

it received the larger right to tax.

With regard to the balance of powers, the passage of time has favored the provinces to such a great extent that contemporary Canada is one of the most decentralized political structures in the world, with every indication that it will so remain. Matters such as education, health, and welfare loom large, so large in fact that provincial responsibility cannot be met by local fiscal capacity, and intergovernmental cost sharing and arrangements for transferring revenue have had to be worked out. Even more significant in the long term has been the grant to the provinces of control over natural resources, for Canada has continued to specialize heavily in staple products. Such money-makers as hydroelectricity in Ontario, Quebec, British Columbia, and Manitoba; oil and gas in Alberta; and potash in Saskatchewan have provided firm economic power bases for these provinces. As for the levying of taxes, both levels of government now have extensive, although often competing, rights; and sharing and cooperation between the federal and provincial governments have become essential.

Canadian federalism has become complex and esoteric: To the structures of the federal government and the provincial governments must be added an array of federal-provincial machinery. There are equalization payments, which are federal transfers of funds to the poorer provinces so that they have, in the terminology of Canada's new Constitution, "sufficient resources to provide reasonably comparable levels of public services and reasonable levels of taxation." Such handouts amounted in the mid-1980s to between one quarter and one third of the total income of the four Atlantic

Provinces. These transfers take some of the edge off the persistent regional disparities that are characteristic of Canada and that are central to how Canadians conceive of their country.

In addition, there are tax-collection agreements by which the federal government both administers and collects income taxes for those provinces that want it to but not for those that do not. In practice, only Quebec, with its propensity to opt out of federal activities, collects personal income tax from its residents, and only Ontario, Quebec, and Alberta collect their own corporate income tax. There are, too, the federal-provincial grants and programs with respect to health and welfare and education. And, in addition, there are innumerable federal-provincial bodies that hold countless meetings. (It has been said that a Canadian is a person who, if asked to choose between free love and a conference on free love, would choose the latter.) At the apex of the whole complex structure stands the annual First Ministers' Conference, for which the prime minister and the 10 premiers assemble and deliberate various federal-provincial matters before a live television audience.

These arrangements are the guts of Canadian federalism—a system that flows from the regionalism and diversity of the nation and aims to confront the underlying economic and social differences among the provinces. To what extent it succeeds is a matter for debate. Regional disparities have persisted, but they have also definitely been alleviated by federal programs. For example, salaries in Canada's poorest province, Newfoundland, are only a little more than half the national average; but when such government transfer payments to individuals as family allowanc-

es and unemployment insurance benefits are added in, a Newfoundlander's personal income rises to almost two thirds the national average. Nevertheless, in comparison with such countries as the United States or Australia, Canada has experienced less growth toward a unified national entity.

One continuing obstacle to unity is the French-English divide. Federalism faced its toughest test when Quebec elected a separatist government in 1976. The referendum, called by Réné

Lévesque's administration during 1980, sought the support of Quebecois for a formula known as "sovereignty-association," meaning an independent Quebec with continuing economic association with the rest of Canada. It is a tribute to the efficacy of Canadian democracy that citizens outside Quebec permitted the issue of separatism to go to a vote and that the 40 percent of those in Quebec who had voted to secede accepted the majority decision with good grace.

109

4

With enhanced rights for the French language both inside and outside the province, Quebecois now feel more secure as Canadians. Yet the future may hold new problems for the province. It is facing net emigration of both Anglophones and Francophones, while its birthrate, once one of the highest in the world, is now among the lowest for any Canadian province. Caught in that demographic squeeze, it could some day find its role within Canada threatened. Although the tide of separatism has ebbed since the defeat of Lévesque's referendum, the long history of Quebec nationalism—which may at times recede but never disappears—suggests that Canadians still cannot afford to become complacent.

In spite of these centrifugal forces, public-opinion polls repeatedly show that Canadians in all regions have a strong emotional commitment to Canada as a nation, which holds the country together; "despite all this diversity, Canada is still a cozy and close-knit country." It is also bound by a web of pan-Canadian institutions. For example, the federal judicial system, headed by the Supreme Court of Canada and now capped by the new Canadian Charter of Rights and Freedoms, and that cliché of Canadiana, the Royal Canadian Mounted Police (RCMP), are two institutions that embody respectively the ideals of law and order.

There is a rare unitary aspect to the Canadian court system: Provincial superior-court judges are federally appointed. But regionalism gets its due at the highest level; traditionally, the nine judges of the Supreme Court of Canada are drawn in the following manner: Three each are appointed from Quebec and Ontario, one comes from the Maritimes, and two come from the

west. Established in 1875 as the highest court in Canada, the Supreme Court did not finally replace the Judicial Committee of Britain's Privy Council as the ultimate court of appeal for all cases until 1949. While most scholars see the decisions of the British judges as having a provincial-rights bias, the Supreme Court strikes most observers as being staunchly federalist.

The Supreme Court took on a new significance for Canadians in 1982 with the entrenchment of a written Charter of Rights and Freedoms in the Constitution. Canadians always had rights that drew, as they still do, on the common law of Great Britain. But the written Canadian Constitution had centered on the distribution of powers between governments, carrying within it the implication that if something could not be done lawfully by one level of government, then it could be done lawfully by the other.

Now the written Constitution has, in the lingo of the politicians, a people's package with a comprehensive list of rights. It commits the federal government to offer language and educational rights to minorities in order to protect Francophones outside Quebec and Anglophones in Quebec. It guarantees all citizens the fundamental freedoms of belief, expression, association, and peaceful assembly, and rights of protection against arbitrary state action. It contains equality clauses for citizens against discrimination on the grounds of race, color, religion, sex, age, or mental or physical disability, and permits affirmative-action programs to remove inequalities. It also makes a bow to provincial autonomy by allowing a province to opt out of its provisions under certain circumstances. There is no doubt that this measure will profound-

ly affect the relationship between individual Canadians and the state, but the details of this new relationship have yet to be established in the courts.

That other great pan-Canadian institution, the RCMP, has also met with changes during recent years. In a fat and informative book written during the 1980s, *New York Times* correspondent Andrew Malcolm observed: "The Mounties are one of three things that Americans think they know about Canada (the other two being Eskimos, who aren't called that anymore, and the Queen, who has never lived there)." Well, the Mounties are still called the Mounties, but it has been a long time since a recruit had to learn how to mount a horse. They are active in a variety of ways all over Canada. As a national police force, they conduct criminal investigations against organized crime, narcotics, and commercial fraud. The Mounties also used to be responsible for security and intelligence, but these functions were shifted to a civilian agency in 1984 after disclosures of illegal activities by the RCMP, including burning a barn suspected of being used for separatist meetings and also stealing membership lists of the Parti Québécois. They are the provincial police force in 8 of the 10 provinces—the exceptions being populous Ontario and Quebec, which are able to support their own police forces—and in the Territories, where the Mounties perform a role similar to that of their forebears on the prairies, mediating between native peoples and the nonnative settlers.

The widespread association of Canadians with the Mounties, a habit of mind not confined to Americans, is sometimes a source of irritation to Canadians, but it is their own fault. "Can-

En route to Vancouver with 108 cars of sulfur, a freight rumbles through Calgary, Alberta. Although it ranks third—after the United States and the Soviet Union—in production, Canada is the leading exporter of the element, which it derives from metallic sulfides and natural gas.

ada must be the only country in the world," says novelist Margaret Atwood, "where a policeman is used as a national symbol"; it is bound to attract attention. In fact, the Mounties have a greater significance for the English than for French Canada; the scarlet tunic was adopted from the British army to suggest the empire and impress the native peoples, and "Royal" was added to the name in 1904 in recognition of the members of the force who had fought alongside the British against the Boers in South Africa.

Beyond the federal and provincial layers of administration in Canada is a third tier: that of local government. The municipalities derive their powers from the provinces, so the systems under which they operate differ from region to region. This diversity has created opportunities for experimentation, and a number of municipalities have shown themselves to be remarkably creative. For example, the establishment in 1953 of metropolitan Toronto—an agglomeration of the city itself and satellite communities such as Etobicoke, North York, and Scarborough—has been hailed as an important breakthrough for urban reform. Since then, it has been much copied throughout North America. Bringing together planning and administration for the entire metropolitan area facilitated rational development, especially in regard to integrated road and public transportation networks. Visiting architects and town planners have dubbed Toronto, with its clean and safe streets, "the city that works," while the older and more sophisticated Montreal continues to be known for its old-world European charm. "Canadians," it was reported in a 1985 Royal Commission on national economic development,

A "nodding donkey" oil pump stands ready near Calmar in Alberta. Discovered in 1910 but not exploited on a significant scale until the late 1940s, the province's oil meets some 85 percent of Canada's demand.

"have been doing something right at the level of local community."

This may seem like more than enough government. Certainly, both Canadians and foreign observers were often inclined to think that way in the 1980s. It is quite true that more than one fifth of working Canadians are employed in the public sector, which accounts for more than two fifths of all income throughout the land. These figures, however, still place Canada only around the average among comparably developed and industrialized countries of the world.

Power is also about making and having money, and if economic success is judged in terms of the benefits it brings to people, Canada's performance since World War II has been distinctly above average. By global standards, the Canadian economy has done well. Comparative data on standards of living invariably put the country near the top of the list. This success is reflected in the good health of Canadians, who have one of the world's highest levels of life expectancy—71.5 years for men, 78.7 for women—and one of the lowest infant mortality rates, at just 1 in 104. Furthermore, the multicultural character of Canada's ethnic peoples bespeaks the widespread attractiveness of the country to other nations; journalist Peter C. Newman, himself an immigrant, has described it in these terms: "To the citizens of most of the world's other countries, Canada appears blessed with the mandate of heaven."

The affluence of the nation today is a tribute to the hard work put in by generations of Canadians, from the settlers who led harsh and bleak lives clearing the land to some immigrants today who work long hours in miserable conditions in the expectation, often realized, that their children will do better. Yet it is equally the product of good fortune. The land has always been rich in food and forests and, as it turned out, there was additional wealth underneath the surface—gold, silver, nickel, lead, zinc, copper, potash, oil, gas, and uranium. Having resources to spare, Canada has been able to sell its surplus to the world, thereby earning foreign exchange to buy the goods produced by other countries in return.

Each province has its own contribution to make to the nation's wealth. The southern parts of Ontario and Quebec have the bulk of the country's industry, while their northern portions have hydroelectric projects such as the great James Bay development in Quebec and mineral deposits such as the huge nickel mines of Sudbury, Ontario. Everywhere, too, there are trees to turn into newsprint. The fisheries, once the foundation of the Canadian economy, still figure largely in the Atlantic Provinces to the east; but they are now joined by the prospect of offshore oil and gas off the coasts of Newfoundland and Nova Scotia.

To the west, the Prairie Provinces used to conjure up visions of endless wheat fields. Now, oil rigs can be added for Alberta, potash mines for Saskatchewan, and hydroelectric dams for Manitoba. West of the Rocky Mountains, British Columbia has the greatest resource wealth in the nation, above all, in its timber. Even the Far North, an area too barren for trees, boasts the minerals of the Canadian Shield, among them lead, zinc, uranium, and tungsten. There is in the Far North, also, some oil and gas onshore, as well as the possibility of an oil and gas bonanza off the coast.

With such riches to back it, Canada has a reasonably well-developed welfare state—one better funded than that of the United States, although less well than Western Europe's—that offers family allowances, old-age security, universal medicare, and unemployment insurance, all paid for through a mildly progressive tax regime. These social safety nets make most Canadians feel more secure; attempts made by financially distraught governments to dismantle programs in the early 1980s met with stout resistance.

Canadians generally look on welfare with a less critical eye than Americans, and in this they reflect a difference in attitude that affects the economy as a whole. Simplistically stated, most Americans fear that the state will do things to them; Canadians expect the state to do things for them. This considerable divergence of opinion among otherwise similar peoples is nowhere more apparent than in the active role the state plays in business life north of the 49th parallel. American observers are invariably struck by the interventionism of the Canadian government.

In its defense, Vancouver commentator Herschel Hardin has called Canada a public enterprise culture and insists that the nation's real entrepreneurship is to be found in the state sector. The list of Crown corporations includes many of the largest and best-known Canadian companies: the Canadian Broadcasting Corporation, Air Canada, Canadian National Railways, Petro-Canada (created in 1975 and within 12 years already one of the largest oil and gas companies in Canada), Ontario Hydro, and Hydro-Quebec. They are the creations of governments at all points on the political spectrum, not only of the Left. The consensus on the acceptability of public ownership was challenged, however, by Brian Mulroney's Conservative administration in the 1980s. Reflecting a worldwide trend toward denationalization, or privatization, his government sold the de Havilland airplane company, acquired as a public enterprise in 1974 from British Hawker Siddeley, to Boeing of the United States. Nevertheless, the Canadian Development Investment Corporation, charged with the sale, had to move cautiously in the face of considerable public opposition.

In general, however, the Canadian tradition has been one in which governments have taken a strong lead in creating national transportation and communications systems and developing resources. From the Canadian Pacific Railway in the 1880s to the off-and-on megaprojects in the energy sector today—mostly off since the collapse of the oil-producing OPEC cartel in the mid-1980s brought prices tumbling down—Canada has been developed by a marriage of public-sector and private-sector endeavors. There has been a fear throughout, justified in the face of dynamic American expansionism, that unless east-west structures were created by the state to hold the country together, Canada would be pulled wholly into a north-south axis dominated by private American capital and risk being torn asunder. The

HARNESSING THE FORCE OF THE WATERS

A dam nearly 2.5 miles long contains the La Grande 3 reservoir.

Water thunders down the spillway of La Grande 3.

Begun in 1971 and running in 1985, the James Bay project in northern Quebec is the largest hydroelectric power plant in Canada and one of the largest in the world. Covering 67,187 square miles, the project diverts water from several rivers to La Grande Rivière, doubling its flow.

Five huge reservoirs were then created, with a total storage capacity of more than 270 billion cubic yards. The lakes feed three powerhouse complexes with 37 generating units that in 1985 provided almost half of the electricity used in Quebec.

The dams are equipped with spillways to act as safety valves in case of unusually high water levels following spring rains. The largest dam (left) is three times the height of Niagara Falls and can discharge a water flow twice that of the St. Lawrence River at Montreal. Its tiers are shaped like ski jumps so that water falls away from the dam.

Although the project has altered the ecology of an area the size of New England and has restricted hunting, its positive consequence has been to reduce the price of electricity in Quebec. The cost per unit is one fifth the price in New York and about half that in France, West Germany, and England.

An electric generator nears completion.

Research equipment dwarfs a worker.

choices, in this view, remain the ones spelled out by public-broadcasting advocate Graham Spry when proselytizing for the creation of the Canadian Broadcasting Corporation in the 1930s: "The States or the state."

Being the product of pragmatism and not ideology, these public enterprises, once created, are usually run in the same way as private enterprises. In the spirit of compromise that is so characteristic of Canada, they are expected, wherever possible, to make their way in competition with rival firms not owned by the state. Hence, Canadian National Railways take on the nonpublic Canadian Pacific; Air Canada competes with CP Air; Canadian Broadcasting Corporation faces the Canadian Television Network (CTV) and Global Television, to say nothing of the American networks flooding in via cable; and Petro-Canada coexists with Exxon's Imperial Oil and British-Dutch Shell.

The interventionist role of the Canadian state, though great, should not be exaggerated, however, for it does have substantial limitations. Competition policy—legislation that is aimed at combating price-fixing agreements and other anticompetitive conduct—has long lacked muscle and has been further weakened by recent decisions of the Supreme Court. For example, the Crown has never won a contested merger case. Tax reform seems invariably to fail in the face of business opposition. All these facts reflect a single truth: Canada is predominantly a business society, and its businessmen wield great influence.

Canada's business class was born, like Canada itself, from the exigencies of producing, gathering, and exporting resources for a succession of great powers—France, Britain, and now the United States. Its greatest strengths still lie more in commerce than industry. But where it is strong, it is exceptionally strong, and its influence can extend beyond Canada's borders. Five Canadian banks, which operate mostly from towering structures of black and glistening gold, dominate the skyline of downtown Toronto. And they cast even longer financial shadows, handling 85 percent of Canadian banking while doing 40 percent of their business outside Canada. Matching them in concentrated economic clout are the nine individuals or families who, according to a study undertaken by the Canadian Bankers' Association, are in control of almost half the shares in the Toronto Stock Exchange's 300 list. Together, these people form a group portrait of the higher echelons of the Canadian business world.

They include the Bronfmans, whose fortune sprang from father Sam's liquor business, which prospered in spite of—even perhaps because of—Prohibition in Canada and the United States. Today, his sons Edgar and Charles run Seagrams, the largest distilling operation in the world; Charles is also the principal owner of the Montreal Expos baseball team. Other club members are the Southams, who own the largest Canadian newspaper chain; Paul Desmarais, who controls the conglomerate Power Corporation; and the Reichmann brothers. The Reichmanns rank among the largest commercial landlords in New York and perhaps among the world's largest developers; their holdings also include Abitibi-Price, the largest newsprint producer in the world, and the recently acquired oil company Gulf Canada.

Also among the nine are two more newspaper magnates: Ken Thomson,

Lumberjacks on Vancouver Island fell a stand of western hemlock. The trees, reaching 330 feet, are now the main lumber species on the west coast, grown for logging and for the pulp and paper industries.

who runs a group of companies that controls Canada's national newspaper, the *Globe and Mail,* as well as the venerable Hudson's Bay Company; and Conrad Black, who used his Canadian-made capital to buy a majority holding in the London *Daily Telegraph* in 1985. In so doing, he followed a tradition set by two earlier Canadians, Max Aitken and Roy Thomson—father of Ken—who both made fortunes in Canada but chose to leave their mark as press barons on Britain's Fleet Street. Aitken was a millionaire at 30, from selling bonds in Canada, when he came to Britain in 1910. He entered politics soon after his arrival; became a newspaper proprietor after World War I; and in World War II, as Lord Beaverbrook, became a key member of Churchill's wartime cabinet, having responsibility for aircraft production. Thomson parlayed a string of radio stations and newspapers in northern Ontario into ownership of *The Times* and *Sunday Times* of London—as well as into substantial holdings in North Sea oil and the title Lord Thomson of Fleet. His tombstone in the crypt of London's St. Paul's Cathedral reads "a strange and adventurous man from nowhere"—which seems rather an odd way to describe Canada.

As some of the names of Canada's reigning economic dynasties suggest, the top echelon of corporate Canada is no longer completely dominated by Anglophones of British ancestry. At long last, Canadian big business has become more open to Francophones and to Anglophones of non-British extraction. However, recent sociological studies, while confirming that trend, show that nothing helps like being born with a silver spoon in one's mouth. Without the advantage of inherited wealth, it remains harder to gain access to the top

in Canada than it is in the United States.

Canadian business has carved out a substantial niche for itself within North America. That much alone can be inferred from the statistics on trade between the two countries—the largest interchange of its kind in the world. A staggering 75 percent of Canadian exports went to the United States in 1985, and 72 percent of imports came from there; in sharp contrast, the figures for trade with the one-time mother country, Britain, were about 2 percent in each case. Canada currently supplies the United States with goods and services ranging from lumber and cement to newsprint and energy. Moreover, Canadian entrepreneurs are heavily involved in such fields as property development and the media.

Some commentators see evidence in this success of a new spirit of confidence in the business community. Canadians can hope that this is so, and time will tell. But extensive Canadian penetration of the American economy is not new; the first serious study of American investment in Canada, published in the 1930s, was entitled *Canadian-American Industry* because of the pervasive two-way investment across the border that it documented. But owing to Canada's heavy dependence on American markets, local business remains the junior partner, notwithstanding its notable achievements.

For a long time, Canadians unconcernedly enjoyed the benefits of American investment in Canada; if there were costs, Canadians were oblivious of them. But as the British Empire went into terminal decline after World War

4

ally increased during the years the Third Option had been in operation. That fact was then used to argue that Canada must secure and enhance the trading connection by negotiating a bilateral free-trade arrangement. Meanwhile, FIRA was renamed Investment Canada and told to start actively soliciting more money from abroad.

In reality, unlike Canada-U.S. trade, the proportion of the Canadian economy under foreign control had peaked in the early 1970s and had fallen significantly thereafter. There was room for doubt, though, about whether FIRA could claim much credit for that. The American financial publication *Barron's*—no friend to government intervention—even claimed that the agency would have been hard put to keep out Murder Inc. Rather, the growth in Canadian ownership seemed the achievement of a more mature Ca-

nadian business class, albeit one operating mostly on the North American rather than the global stage. The same inference might be drawn from the fate of the National Energy Program. A spurt in Canadianization until the summer of 1982 was followed by a lull when nationalist measures were generally being put on hold. The gains made previously were not rolled back, however, and the Canadian takeover of Gulf Canada by private interests in the mid-1980s showed that Canadian capital had acquired muscle.

On balance, then, the 1970s and early 1980s saw Canada increasingly linked to the United States in terms of trade but marginally more the master in its own house in terms of the ownership of industry. This last trend was evident in the labor movement. From the origins of unionization in Canada in the mid-19th century, Canadian work-

ers had tended to be affiliated with branches of labor unions based in the United States. The result was what was known as "international unions"— though in fact they were, like the World Series, merely continental. Unkind critics preferred to call them American unions operating in Canada. Their logic for Canadian members lay initially in the way they facilitated a cross-frontier labor movement. Holding the same union card as their American fellows, workers could move from Toronto to Buffalo, New York, or to wherever jobs were, without regard to the border. Then, as American branch plants came to Canada, the international unions seemed to hold out the promise of higher wages for the native work force. In the telling words of Samuel Gompers, the first head of the American Federation of Labor, for whom it was evident that American capital had come to Canada to oppress Canadian workers: "When the Yankee capitalist did this, it was but natural that the Yankee 'agitator' should follow him."

Since the mid-1960s, however, the situation has radically changed. There has been an unprecedented number of Canadian breakaways from international unions. The process culminated in the spectacular exit of more than 100,000 Canadians from the international United Auto Workers to form their own independent union during a dispute with General Motors in the mid-1980s.

The reason for the defections lies in the greater militancy of the Canadian work force over recent years. In the mid-1950s, the unionized proportion of the labor force in each country was about the same, at 30 percent. Since then, the Canadian ratio has risen to almost 40 percent and is still rising, while the American figure has fallen to below 20 percent. In such circumstances, not surprisingly, American workers have been more inclined to be quiescent and to make concessions to their employers than their Canadian counterparts, and American unions no longer set an example for Canadian workers to emulate.

A contributory factor has been the increasing strength of the public-sector unions, which have been growing at a time when the industrial unions have remained static or have shrunk. Overwhelmingly, these unions are national rather than international; what government is prepared to have its civil servants at the beck and call of foreign union bosses? So, relatively speaking, the long-dominant international unions have dwindled. By 1980, and for the first time since reliable counts have been made, the majority of Canadian workers were in unions whose headquarters are in Canada.

One notable side effect of the Canadianization of the labor movement has been to give a firmer popular base to Canadian nationalism. The unions headed the opposition to bilateral free trade in the 1980s, providing a counterweight to the integrative impulse of the business community.

The 1980s raised many problems for Canadians, as the decade did for much of the world. The inflation of the 1970s was mostly brought under control, although high levels of unemployment persisted. Seasonal layoffs remained a

Agricultural workers plant rows of celery at a farm in the Holland district of Ontario, north of Toronto. The area was once a marsh; since it was drained in the 1920s, it has become one of Canada's most prosperous vegetable-growing regions.

plague; in the Newfoundland outports, for example, well over half of the working-age population was usually without a job in the winter. Canada was a resource economy and, over the long term, had done well for itself; but it suffered when resource prices sagged in times of recession. The collapse of the OPEC oil cartel, for example, was good news for consumers worldwide but bad news for oil-producing Canada, where major energy projects that had been counted on to get the economy going were put on indefinite hold. Although the nation could boast a substantial industrial base to supplement its resources, the quality of its manufacturing firms left something to be desired in a world of intense competition and rapid technological change.

The bottom line for Canada, though, was the American connection. Here, Canada was between the proverbial rock and a hard place. Economic imperatives were pushing Canada toward yet fuller integration in a North American version of a common market. But such a course was fraught with political risks: the further loss of control in most economic matters and the erosion of a distinctive political culture.

The challenge that is facing Canada today is as old as the country: How to survive as a separate political entity on the northern half of the North American continent—how, in a colorful analogy of Pierre Trudeau's, a mouse is to coexist with an elephant. In the unequal division of power involved, Canada may seem to have little room for maneuver. But it does not hurt to remind Canadians that there are choices to be made. And the more limited scope they may have to influence events, the more important it becomes to make the necessary decisions wisely.   □

Wheat surrounds a silo in Saskatchewan, the center of grain production in Canada. Covering some 24.7 million acres in the early 1980s, when the harvests averaged over 20 billion long tons, wheat is the main crop on 20 percent of the nation's farms.

THE NOBLE ART OF THE WEST COAST INDIANS

In 1778, when England's master mariner Captain James Cook landed on the unexplored shores of what is now British Columbia, he was met by a surprise: an unknown but highly developed Indian culture whose every object, however utilitarian, was made with style and artistry. Living in an abundant but inaccessible region, tribes such as the Haida, Kwakiutl, and Tsimshian were heir to a centuries old tradition of fine craftsmanship. The tradition continues and has led to their masks, amulets, and other artifacts being ranked among the world's most prized examples of ethnic art.

The Indians themselves, however, never hoarded their goods for their material value. For them, the one sure way to win public esteem was to give such things away at great festivals—called potlatches—that served as monuments to the host tribe's munificence.

Totem poles depicting mythic family histories crowd a 19th-century Haida village (*above*). The restored totems to the left and right now stand in Vancouver's Stanley Park.

124

Thirty inches long, this wooden ladle decorated with a carved fish and an eagle's head was used to transfer huge quantities of fish, game, and fruit into serving dishes at potlatches. A feast might last for a week and draw several hundred guests.

The stylized heads of a whale *(left)* and an eagle *(right)* stare from opposite ends of a potlatch dish carved in the 1890s. The largest vessels were almost 20 feet long; from these the food was scooped into smaller bowls like this one, which served up to half a dozen guests.

Inlaid with abalone shell, this chest made of cedarwood guarded a family's most-treasured possessions. The Indians made the body by kerfing—grooving—a single plank of wood, steaming it until it was pliable, then bending it into shape and sewing the edges together with cedar roots.

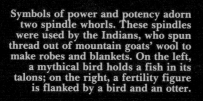

Symbols of power and potency adorn two spindle whorls. These spindles were used by the Indians, who spun thread out of mountain goats' wool to make robes and blankets. On the left, a mythical bird holds a fish in its talons; on the right, a fertility figure is flanked by a bird and an otter.

A wooden headdress that was used in Kwakiutl dance ceremonies represents the mythic Thunderbird, a powerful spirit from whose beak, the Indians claimed, lightning flashed. Its masked impersonator in the celebrations imitated bird movements to the rhythm of singing and drums.

A Haida artist from the Queen Char-
lotte Islands off the coast of British
Columbia carved this boldly decorated dance mask. Such portraits rarely
recorded the visages of living people;
instead, they were intended to
depict familiar spirits or ancestors
featured in the ceremonies.

Carved from wood, this winged frog
served to top a masked dancer's head-
piece. Supernatural transformations
of animals and people were central to
most Pacific Coast Indian myths,
which in turn provided the themes on
which the rituals were based.

These bone objects are two of the shaman's tools for combating sickness. The soul-catcher *(top)* retrieved a patient's spirit, thought to leave the body during illness, so it could effect a cure. The amulet *(bottom)* depicts the crane-spirit from which the healer drew his powers.

A Tsimshian chief once wore this eagle frontlet as the centerpiece of a headdress trimmed with ermine. The abalone shell used for inlays in this and other objects came from Mexico, 1,875 miles away to the south, and was brought up the coast by traders.

A giant mural showing an archetypal beach scene looms above a child in the Quebec town of Hull. Dreams of the sun draw many Canadians south during the long winters; each year some two million visit Florida alone.

A SEPARATE IDENTITY

Canadians have sometimes been referred to as "decaffeinated Americans": Brewed from the same beans, with the same flavor, but not likely to keep you awake at night. This kind of description makes nationalist Canadians writhe with indignation. "We are *not* Americans," they insist, "and we have plenty of cultural vitality and excitement." On the surface, though, there is much evidence to support the notion of similarity, particularly in the fields of leisure and material culture.

The fact is that, to outsiders, Canadians can easily be mistaken for their neighbors south of the border. They dress like Americans; their cars, food, houses, and plumbing are in the American mold; and many of them work in industries that are largely owned by Americans. Their eating habits have been strongly influenced by hundreds of McDonald's fast-food franchises. In Toronto and Montreal, Canadians troop out loyally to the major-league baseball games and boo the New York Mets and Yankees as enthusiastically as fans in Chicago or Los Angeles. And Canadian football fans make much of the differences between their game and the U.S. version, though to an outsider these amount to subtleties rather than matters of substance, with the Canadian field being larger and the game being played 12 instead of 11 to a side.

The odds are, too, that Canadians vacationing outside the country will spend their time in the United States; one quarter of foreign trips made by Canadians take them south of the border, and on any day in January or February, 4 percent of the population will be enjoying the sun in Florida.

The look and layout of a Toronto newspaper is almost indistinguishable from its equivalent in New York. To foreigners, so are the Canadian and American accents. For French Canadians, language is a bulwark against cultural imports; but when English Canadians switch on the television, they watch U.S. programs for 75 percent of their viewing time. Fully 97 percent of the dramas they watch originate in the United States.

Yet important and deeply rooted distinctions between Canadians and Americans do exist. Canadians are—if there is any truth in the popular stereotypes—more circumspect, conservative, and reserved than Americans, qualities often ascribed to the puritanism of their Calvinist and Jansenist ancestors. Canadians reveal their caution in quantifiable ways. They invest less in their own economy than Americans but save twice as much; and although their public health service is wider ranging than that of their neighbors to the south, they take out more insurance than any other people in the world. In the words of Canadian writer Margaret Atwood: "The Canadian mind-set is skeptical-ironic, the American idealistic-optimistic. Praise an American and he'll agree with you;

5

praise a Canadian and he'll think you're trying to sell him something."

This sentiment is reflected in the Canadian attitude toward leisure, which has historically been one of suspicion. Things are changing; the old gibe that Canadians roll up the sidewalks in Toronto on Sundays no longer catches the spirit of a city whose cafés, restaurants, art galleries, and parks are jammed on the weekends. Nevertheless, compared with Australians or Americans, Canadians are not conspicuously hedonistic; if they no longer regard loafing around or enjoying themselves as sinful, neither do they consider it a natural right.

A crucial factor that stops Canadians from behaving like the citizens of Australia or of the United States is climate. As it always has, Winter with a capital *W* remains the presiding arbiter of much that Canadians do or avoid. Almost everywhere, the season is long and harsh; only on Vancouver Island, with its temperate, almost English weather pattern, do a few fortunate souls insist that there, at least, General Winter is not in command.

Winter could even be said to define the pleasures of the summer months; the methodical way in which many people plan their vacations and weekends from June through August is based less on anticipated pleasure than on ensuring that not one precious moment of good weather is wasted. For most Canadians, summer is the only time that they can get away and enjoy the huge tracts of land and water that surround them. No other country in the world has so much wilderness within easy reach of its main urban centers, and there are few Canadians who fail to take advantage of their precious heritage. This remains true despite the ubiquitous mosquitoes and other biting

In British Columbia, near the Alberta border, canoeists paddle gently across a lake shrouded in early-morning mist. Canoeing is one of the nation's most popular summertime recreations, offering enthusiasts the chance to explore the country's unrivaled network of lakes and rivers.

A poster issued by Ontario's Ministry of Natural Resources marks a portage, or overland route, used to bypass waterfalls or rapids. Many of Canada's portage trails were blazed by Indians, whose open birchwood boats were the prototypes of the vessel now known as the Canadian canoe.

insects that are the bane of the Canadian outdoors, particularly in early summer, when the bitter, astringent taste of mosquito repellent inadvertently sprayed on the lips becomes one of the characteristic seasonal flavors.

The pattern of settlement in Canada means that the "bush"—as Canadians call the wilderness—is never far away. The layout works concentrically; cities are surrounded by suburbs, which in turn give way to farm country, beyond which the bush awaits. The land there is so empty that it can seem to belong to each of its visitors personally, as though no other person had ever set eyes on it. That sentiment is heightened by the fact that great areas of government survey maps carry no labels. Thousands of the country's roughly two million lakes have yet to be named, and it used to be said that one could tag a lake simply by sending a suitable fee to the relevant government inspector in Ottawa.

For many Canadians, going into the bush means a boat trip. More than half the population—about 13 million people—go boating each year in a virtual armada of almost 2.3 million boats, more than twice the number per capita to be found in the United States. Canadians spend two billion dollars on the purchase and maintenance of these vessels each year: It is not unusual to meet people who have spent more on their boats than on their houses.

A panoramic survey of Canadians afloat during the summertime should start in St. John's, Newfoundland, at the annual Regatta Day, which is always held toward the end of June. It is the oldest such event in North America. Here, the city's brawniest youths assemble to race rowing sculls across Quidi Vidi—a pond in local parlance, but a fine freshwater lake by the standards of

less aquatic nations. Along the coasts of the Maritime Provinces, sailboats are much in evidence—from sleek 65-foot ketches crewed by the wealthy old families of Halifax to lowly dinghies and snipes off Dalhousie Sound on New Brunswick's Chaleur Bay. Although outboard-motor boats are the preferred leisure craft of cottagers and weekenders in Quebec and Ontario, the traditionally styled open canoe is still a common sight—especially at the hundreds of summer camps to which more than one million Canadian children are dispatched each year so that they may enjoy the wilderness and escape parental scrutiny.

The Prairie Provinces, with their great plains and their traditional allegiance to the soil, might not seem like boating country, but in fact Manitoba, Saskatchewan, and Alberta all possess intricate and extensive lake and river systems. Winnipeggers have Lake Winnipeg and Lake Manitoba to explore; fleets of kayaks ply the long Qu'Appelle River north of Regina; and there are dozens of lakes within easy reach of Edmonton. All along the breathtaking shoreline of British Columbia, boats are a way of life—not just for the many fishermen in the province but also for the well-heeled yachting enthusiasts who are attracted to one of the world's finest coasts.

In all these provinces, Canadians are following the tradition laid down by their pioneering ancestors, who in turn learned their boating skills from the Indians and Inuit. It was the native peoples who first explored the seemingly unending waterways, and on many of the hard-to-reach rivers and lakes they remain the only authorities. Anyone traveling to the Yukon or to the Northwest Territories will discover that boats still play a major role in local transportation. In these regions, however, there is less romance about the traditional canoe and kayak than there is among the city-bred dwellers to the south, who may still get misty-eyed at the sound of a paddle dipping into the clear waters of a remote lake at dusk.

Such sights and sounds are common in Canada's 28 national parks, which attracted almost 20 million visitors in 1985. The national park system was started in 1885 with a 10-square-mile reservation around the hot mineral springs in what is now Alberta's Banff National Park. Since then, the amount of land throughout Canada set apart for public recreation and for conservation has risen to nearly 50,000 square miles—less than 2 percent of the total landmass, but an area roughly the size of England. In addition to these na-

5

tional parks, there are more than 1,000 parks that are run by provincial governments, the biggest of them nearly 12,000 square miles in extent.

Most national parks offer various recreational activities, among them hiking, climbing, swimming, canoeing, snowshoeing, and bird and animal watching. Hunting is prohibited, but fishing is permitted, and many of the lakes are stocked. Camping is the most popular leisure activity, and as visitors enter each park they are handed details of sites and trails, along with instructions covering such emergencies as what to do in the event of a forest fire or an unexpected encounter with a bear. Older parks, such as Banff, are provided with hotels, which are prohibited in newer parks where the emphasis is on preserving the tranquillity and beauty of some of the world's most magnificent scenery and its wildlife.

Less celebrated, but equally rewarding to visit, are Canada's 80 national historic parks and sites, the first of which was established at Fort Anne in Annapolis Royal in 1917. Taken as a whole, they provide a comprehensive overview of the nation's history. In Quebec City, the Cartier-Brébeuf Park marks Jacques Cartier's first winter camp as well as the site of the Jesuit order's first residence in Canada. The subsequent economy of the country can be followed by visiting a series of sites that have associations with the fur trade—Indian, French, and British. Military history is celebrated at the massive French fortress of Louisburg on Cape Breton Island, painstakingly reconstructed, as well as at such places as Fort Rodd Hill on Vancouver Island, the site of the British coastal defenses in the 19th century. In addition, there are collections of old buildings uprooted

from their original locations and gathered together in places such as Heritage Park in Calgary and the Acadian Historical Village outside Caraquet, in New Brunswick.

Although hunting is forbidden in the parks and preserves, it is a major sport elsewhere, pursued by more than one million Canadians who, in the 1986 season, accounted for the killing of at least 880,000 grouse, 248,000 white-tailed deer, 102,000 caribou, 63,000 moose, 25,000 mule deer, and 20,000 black bears. The list does not cover the controversial practice of sealing; that trade, the focus of international criticism in the 1970s, is a matter of commerce and culling, not sport. Moose and bear, however, do attract many international big-game hunters, who sometimes spend thousands of dollars to be flown to remote camps in the northern hinterland for a week's stay. To the distaste of those Canadians who are opposed to killing for sport, some of the more boisterous members of the hunting fraternity celebrate their prowess by cruising around their hometowns bearing their prey mounted on their car roofs.

Hunting also thrives on a less exalted plane. On countless farms across the nation, smaller game—especially rabbits—have given many a youngster a start in hunting skills. The most skilled hunters are native Canadians, many of whom not only still make their living as guides or escorts for hunting parties but also provide their families with a substantial part of their protein intake from hunting, trapping, and fishing. The duck-hunting season gets an enthusiastic turnout, and traditional duck decoys, often carved by native artisans, are considered works of art in many nonhunting homes.

In Alberta's Banff National Park, a hotel stands wedged between conifers and Bow Lake, whose waters are fed by surrounding glaciers. Founded in 1885, Banff was Canada's first national park; now its scenery, wildlife, and amenities draw three million vacationers each year.

In a game for the coveted trophy, the Stanley Cup, red-shirted Montreal Canadiens clash with opponents from New York. Developed in its present form in Canada in the 19th century, ice hockey is now the country's most popular spectator sport.

The end of the hunting season coincides with the onset of winter. The first heavy snowfalls transform the appearance of Canadians on the streets. For the next six months, they look like well-padded Martians in their thick, down-filled parkas and enormous snow boots. Canadians have long experience in dressing for winter, but they are always on the lookout for new ways of combating the cold. One year, they may be using chemical hand warmers—little plastic containers that are kept inside a glove or coat pocket and twisted to give off heat. Another year, the fad may call for Canadians to try a new snowboot design or a "revolutionary" synthetic insulating material for clothing.

Many urban Canadians are committed to sheltering from the cold—a commitment made increasingly tangible with the construction of miles of covered shopping malls, often tunneling down deep beneath the city streets. Some of these complexes are so cavernous that they feel like the outdoors, complete with gardens, trees, terraces, cafés, and waterfalls.

The apotheosis of these developments is in Edmonton, which in the mid-1980s claimed to have the largest indoor complex in the world, a megamall eight city blocks long and three blocks wide. The facilities include a skating rink large enough for the Edmonton Oilers to practice on, an artificial lake with wave machines for surfing and waterskiing, and a second body of water with sharks that can be viewed from four submarines—which number, as people say, four more than the Canadian navy has. Economically, the entire population of Alberta is insufficient to support the mall, which seeks to attract visitors from all over Canada and the adjoining American states.

The rabbit warren of passageways and facilities underlying the major Canadian cities has transformed the way of life of many urbanites, who simply used to hibernate if there was no com-

138

pelling need to venture outdoors in winter. Nowadays, though, a retired businessman in Toronto, for example, can leave his apartment in the north of the city to run errands during a blizzard without taking his overcoat. Using his special tenant's key, he gains access to an adjoining shopping mall, itself connected to a subway entrance. Catching a train, he can go to his downtown bank to clip his coupons, visit his stockbroker, pay off his son's parking ticket at City Hall, pick up his new golf clubs (for his approaching "sun holiday" in Florida), arrive exactly on time at his indoor tennis club to play an 11 a.m. doubles match with three other club members, join his wife for lunch at the Royal York Hotel, and get back home for an afternoon nap before catching the early show at his favorite movie theater—and all without stepping out of temperature-controlled comfort. At home once more, he can watch the weather report on television after the national news and congratulate himself on how well he has managed to avoid what many Canadians feel is the "unending curse" of their winter.

The curse is, of course, a blessing to many younger and more athletic Canadians, to whom the first snowfall is the signal for a search-and-rescue operation for last year's skates, skis, toboggans, and hockey sticks. Hockey in Canada means the nation's winter obsession, ice hockey.

Canada's love affair with hockey is one of the most genuinely distinctive features of the country. Hockey is much more than just a game: It is at the core of the national mythology. Most Canadian men who are over the age of 30 grew up listening to play-by-play commentaries on their transistor radios. In the small mining towns of north-

ern Ontario and in the snowbound villages of Quebec, where the great hockey players are born, fabled places such as the Montreal Forum and Maple Leaf Gardens were the Canadian equivalent of Mecca or Valhalla. To skate on that glistening white ice, wearing a Canadien's uniform, take a pass from Maurice "Rocket" Richard and slam it past goaltender Jacques Plante—these were the stuff of Canadian boyhood dreams.

Even though the National Hockey League has expanded to include such cities as warm-weather Los Angeles, the game still encapsulates most Canadian men's images of grace, power, beauty, and aggression. It is also a rich source of national pride—or humiliation. The nation's anguish in the sport is that its greatest players are precluded by their professional status from playing for the team that represents the nation at the Olympic Games. Instead, the national side is made up of junior players who are regularly beaten by the Czechs and Russians; since the early 1960s, the Canadians have won only one silver medal. Quadrennially, then, grim resignation and morbid self-loathing sweep the nation as the Olympic squad heads out again to defeat. Conversely, traffic came to a stop and strangers hugged each other in the street when a team of all-star professionals from the National Hockey League beat the Russians in an eight-game series in 1972.

The competitive urge in hockey is instilled at an early age. Sometimes it seems as if half the families in the land are geared to getting little boys—and an increasing number of little girls—dressed up in protective shoulder and leg pads to skate around a rink from morning to night. There is a continent-

wide infrastructure of hockey leagues for young players—"pee wee," midget, junior, senior, and others; and a child's progression from one to another can occupy much of the family's spare time.

The spectacle of a hockey mother in full war cry in a small-town arena urging on her 10-year-old is not for the fainthearted. The intensity of the competition has to be seen to be believed, and the sacrifices that parents make in their own social lives to ensure that their children get the maximum amount of ice time is also impressive. Most parents realize that their offspring are not destined to play professional hockey; and indeed, most would not want them to. There are others, however, who know that scouts for the big teams haunt the senior league games, looking for candidates to be signed up for the semiprofessional leagues from which the select band of hockey heroes are ultimately chosen. The suspected presence of a scout at a young players' league game only serves to fuel the frenzied exhortations of ambitious parents cheering on their young hopefuls.

Skiing, both downhill and cross-country, is even more popular than hockey as a participation sport, attracting some five million Canadians. Downhill is the more glamorous sport, but a significant number of enthusiasts have left the crowded and expensive mountains, lured by cross-country skiing. Since the beginning of the 1980s, even the downhill clubs themselves have opened up extensive marked trails to cater to the growing demand.

Many of the cross-country skiers, however, prefer to find their own routes. They are a particular breed: appreciative of nature, responsive to challenges, and also extremely fit. Un-

5

Skiers dropped off by helicopter on the almost inaccessible slopes of the Cariboo Mountains leave the undulating pattern of their progress in virgin snow. The use of helicopters has opened vast terrain for wealthy sports enthusiasts in search of adventure and unspoiled landscapes.

fortunately, many of their favorite locations also attract legions of snowmobile fanatics, and these two groups are mutually antagonistic. To cross-country skiers, dangerous and noisy snowmobiles are akin to bats out of hell; to the machines' riders, skiers are self-righteous cranks.

Not surprisingly, winter sports furnish most of Canada's sporting heroes, and any Olympic gold-medal winner is automatically idolized. Thus Gaetan Boucher, a young and unknown speed skater hailing from Quebec, entirely changed the public's attitude toward his sport after his Winter Olympics win in 1984. Where once there had been only three or four speed-skating rinks in the entire country, there are now more than a dozen.

If winter for sports fans means hockey or skiing, then summer means baseball. Canadians used to have an ambivalent attitude toward the sport, avidly following the games in the big United States leagues but ridiculing the idea of a "World Series" that included only American teams. In 1969, however, the Montreal Expos were admitted into the U.S. National Baseball League, and a decade later, it was the Toronto Blue Jays' turn to enter the American Baseball League. In Ontario and Quebec at least, baseball fanaticism became the order of the day, despite the fact that most of the players in the two top teams are Americans and Puerto Ricans. Because they play in different leagues, the two squads do not normally meet, except for one game a year, which is played for the Pearson Cup, a trophy named after former prime minister Lester Pearson, whose greatest passion was baseball.

Other sports in which Canadians have recently excelled include pool, where Cliff Thorburn is a one-time world champion and holder of the record number of maximum breaks; and swimming, with Alex Baumann, a double gold-medal winner at the 1984 Los Angeles Olympic Games. But perhaps the nation's greatest long-term contribution to world sports has been its national inventiveness in devising new games. Canadian sports innovators range from the Algonquin Indians of the St. Lawrence valley, credited with originating lacrosse, to one James Naismith, a Presbyterian clergyman who in 1891 drew up the rules of basketball while working as a physical-education instructor in the United States. Canadians even played a role in the evolution of American football, through the pivotal games played between Harvard University and Montreal's McGill University in 1874.

The picture of Canada as a sporting nation is borne out by statistics in which 56 percent of Canadians claim to be classed as physically active, to the extent of doing some form of exercise for at least three hours a week. (People walk and swim a lot: Larger towns have public swimming pools.) This percentage needs to be balanced, however, by images of Canadians engaged in less physically demanding leisure pursuits. For instance, eating out has been steadily growing in popularity. Fast-food outlets, most of them local franchises of the big U.S. chains, are ubiquitous; but in recent years, there has also been a proliferation of gourmet restaurants, many of them run by immigrants from countries where cooking is a serious business. Recently, too, training programs for restaurateurs and chefs have been brought to colleges throughout the country, and the first fruits of this policy are now becoming evident in

a wider and more gastronomically aware selection of eating places.

The Mecca of Canadian gastronomes is Montreal, a city famed for its night-life, and whose downtown restaurant and night-club area can be clogged with traffic as late as 3 a.m. Torontonians used to say dismissively that the difference between them and the Montrealers was that they took their paychecks to the bank on Friday while in Montreal people took them to the bistro, café, or restaurant. But the Montrealers have had the last laugh in the vast influx of tourist dollars their restaurants currently bring in, as well as in the socially useful role that cafés have played in rehabilitating some down-at-the-heel areas of the inner city. Running a starred restaurant has a social cachet now; Jean Drapeau owned Le Vaisseau d'Or when he was mayor of the city. Toronto itself has recently experienced a restaurant boom, and now it offers a wide selection of foreign cuisines, especially Greek, Italian, Chinese, and East European.

Canadian drinking habits are not easy to define, mainly because regulations concerning the sale and consumption of liquor vary from province to province. In Ontario, for example, beer cannot be bought in the same place as wine, although wine can be bought with spirits. In British Columbia, beer cannot be drunk in public, and bars have separate doors for men and women—though such restrictions are largely ignored. In Saskatchewan, a man who buys liquor cannot stop on his journey home, or he will be guilty of committing an offense.

Such restrictive regulations are a legacy of puritanical attitudes that, until recently, informed many aspects of Canadian life, including gambling. Until

At summer festivals across the nation, an array of contests celebrate Canada's rural heritage. They include *(top to bottom)* log rolling on Vancouver Island; a Nova Scotia ox pull, in which oxen must haul heavy weights; and a B.C. sawing competition.

142

the late 1960s, a lottery, for example, was considered something low and sleazy. One bought a ticket to the Irish Sweepstakes illegally, from touts in bars. Then the Canadian government and many of the provincial governments decided that they were foolish to ignore this voluntary tax. The result was a plethora of sweepstake schemes, making lottery mania into a Canadian phenomenon, with 20 to 25 percent of the population regularly buying tickets. In 1984, when one of the lotteries offered a kitty totaling—thanks to a string of nonwinners—more than $12 million (Canadian), it seemed for a few days as though the national psyche had come completely unstuck.

Ticket holders are avid viewers of the weekly lottery television shows, which present a package of light entertainment to hold viewer interest for the big moment when the winning numbers are chosen. Poor cultural fare though they may be, the shows at least have a guaranteed audience, unlike most of the other home-produced Canadian television programs, which face overwhelming competition from American offerings. With the introduction of cable television and satellite dish receivers, there are now few Canadians who cannot tune in to the entire spectrum of American programming. In Toronto, for example, a cable subscriber has access to a dozen Canadian stations and about 20 U.S. stations at any time of day. The result is that more than 80 percent of the entertainment and sports programs watched by Anglophone Canadians in the early 1980s were of foreign—and mostly American—origin. The figure is half this in French-speaking Quebec.

Despite the apparently impossible challenge of competing with the big

Canada's winter carnival contests range from the traditional to the zany. Here *(top to bottom)*, a Toronto crew races a boat over frozen Lake Ontario; contestants in Montreal push a bed over ice; and in Ottawa, spectators watch a dogsled race.

On fashionable downtown Crescent Street, Montrealers relax in a split-level café converted from an old townhouse. The city's French heritage is reflected in its 2,000-plus restaurants and bistros as well as in a taste—weather permitting—for outdoor eating and drinking.

American networks, Canada has developed and maintained a respected publicly owned national television and radio system called the Canadian Broadcasting Corporation (CBC). Created in the 1930s, the CBC controls one of the most geographically dispersed national networks in the world, linking local stations as distant as the remote Arctic, the shores of the Atlantic, and Vancouver Island on the Pacific Coast. In typical Canadian fashion, it balances national network programming with strong regional input.

Canadian broadcasting is also distinguished by the national commitment to provide services in both English and French. Once confined exclusively to Quebec and some areas of French-speaking New Brunswick, the French network of the CBC has been progressively extended across most of the country—sometimes arousing the hostility of local viewers. Nonetheless, a small proportion of the English-speaking population—particularly in central Canada—regularly tunes in to French-language television, and the quality of the programming has won the service grudging admiration even from the staunchest Anglophones.

Typical of many Canadian institutions, the CBC is in other respects something of a British-American hybrid. Just under half its revenues are subsidized by the taxpayer in the form of government grants, while the rest of the funding comes from advertising. This irritates the privately owned networks and stations, which feel that the CBC receives an unfair advantage by competing for commercial revenue without needing to be profitable. Defenders of the system say that it is a necessary compromise if Canada is to retain a truly national network; the

government cannot carry the entire financial burden, and Canadians have rejected the British solution of charging consumers an annual license fee.

From time to time, various Canadian governments have attempted to reduce the level of American television imports. In 1970, for example, the Canadian Parliament passed legislation compelling all Canadian networks to ensure that 60 percent of their output was Canadian in origin. Standards for the CBC are even stricter: At least 70 percent of its television programs and more than 80 percent of its radio programs are supposed to be of local origin. This raises the question of what constitutes "Canadian." For instance, should Oscar Peterson or Neil Young, both native Canadians, performing on an American show purchased by a Canadian network, count as Canadian content? Only a bureaucrat knows for sure. And confronted by so much bureaucracy, the two main private networks—Canadian Television Network and Global—have become adept at finding loopholes in the law. The popular and undeniably American Western series, *Bonanza*, was once passed off as Canadian content on the grounds that the lead actor, Lorne Greene, was born in Ottawa.

Some genuinely local programs have proved highly successful at home and abroad. Canadian soap operas can have

5

a down-to-earth realism and humanity that distinguishes them from the Hollywood equivalent; one, *The Plouffe Family,* based on the novels of Quebecois author Roger Lemelin, was a legendary success with both Francophone and Anglophone audiences during the 1950s. And one-shot drama specials can do even better: *Anne of Green Gables* (based on the novels of Lucy Maud Montgomery) attracted the largest number of viewers in Canadian history when it was shown in 1985.

In the same way, government intervention has helped maintain a national magazine industry, although not without some controversy over the methods used. In 1975, tax concessions were withdrawn from the Canadian editions of *Time* and *Reader's Digest,* because they were thought to be soaking up too much local advertising revenue at the expense of Canadian-owned publications. *Time's* Canadian edition subsequently shut down operations, though *Reader's Digest* managed to adapt to the new situation and survived. The immediate beneficiaries of the measure were the Canadian magazines *Saturday Night,* which resumed publication following a year's closure, and *Macleans,* which was revamped as a newsmagazine. Since then, both have flourished, a fact that many Canadians believe to have vindicated the government's action. In recent years, however, the main direction of the industry has been away from general-interest magazines and toward more specialized types of publication—a tendency that is also strongly evident in the United States.

One area in which the government has no need to intervene is the newspaper industry. The vastness of the country has made widespread distribution difficult for dailies, so the pattern

that has developed has been one of local papers covering primarily neighborhood news. In recent years, the trend has been toward chain ownership, the Thomson and Southam chains being the biggest. The days of the small, independently owned newspaper seem numbered, though there are still a few fine survivors, such as the Kingston *Whig Standard.* Canada has one national newspaper, the Toronto *Globe and Mail,* owned by the Thomson organization. With Thomson's huge resources behind it, the *Globe and Mail* beats the distance problem by operating a chain of satellite printing plants across the country that offer same-day delivery of a national edition in every province. In terms of circulation, however, the *Globe and Mail* is outclassed by *The Toronto Star,* the biggest-selling newspaper, which competes for readership with the feisty and often saucy *Toronto Sun.*

Although Canadians remain avid newspaper readers, their loyalty is not unwavering. They read newspapers out of habit, and when the habit is altered—especially by a long strike, as happened in Montreal and Vancouver at the end of the 1970s—it becomes very difficult to regain readership. The Montreal *Star,* for instance, which had been losing readers even before the stike, never recovered. Although it had once been the largest-circulation English-language daily in Quebec, the newspaper had to fold its tent a few months after the strike.

The economic saving grace for most newspapers in Canada has been the introduction of new computer technology, which has reduced production costs dramatically. A decade before the new equipment actually arrived, the stage was set with the failure of major print-

union strikes against all three Toronto dailies. Weakened by that defeat, the unions were unable to put up a strong resistance to the new machines; in contrast to the convulsions that afflicted the British newspaper business during 1985 and 1986, Canada accepted the new computer technology in the mid-1970s with scarcely a whimper.

The factors that have most affected the development of Canada's media—the geographical dispersion and the joint French-English presence—have also exerted a profound influence on high culture. The existence of Quebec has ensured that two separate cultural traditions and identities have always co-existed within the nation, each with relatively little awareness of what the other was doing. As for geography, the great distances that separate Canada's population centers have encouraged the growth of several different cultural centers, rather than a single focal point such as Paris or London.

The great rivals in this respect, as in many others, are Toronto and Montreal. Both have all the appurtenances of modern institutional culture: theaters, symphony orchestras, opera companies, and ballet troupes. Toronto has the edge in regard to the last two categories; it is the home of the National Ballet of Canada, the country's largest professional company, as well as of the leading producer of lyric drama, the Canadian Opera Company. Montreal would claim a slightly larger intellectual community, based on the presence of its four universities—two French-speaking and two English-speaking, including the celebrated McGill—as well as a spectacular arts center, the Place des Arts, with three auditoriums and its own resident

In Vancouver's Chinatown, a mother carrying her child in a sling chooses vegetables from a market stall. The district, which was established in the 1880s, has 30,000 inhabitants, making it the second-largest Chinese community in North America; only San Franciso's Chinatown is larger.

orchestra, the Montreal Symphony. Some people, too, like the way that English and French cultures happily rub shoulders in Montreal.

While Canada's two largest cities are natural centers for the performing arts, the most remarkable growth in cultural activities has taken place far from the main metropolitan centers, in Winnipeg. "Miles from nowhere," as the early settlers used to say, Winnipeggers decided early on that they did not intend to live in a cultural desert. So they established the Royal Winnipeg Ballet in 1938, the oldest ballet company in Canada, though it gained international prominence only in the 1960s, under the energetic direction of Arnold Spohr. The Winnipeg Symphony Orchestra and the Manitoba Theater Center, created in 1958 as the first of Canada's professional regional theaters, complete a trio that have made the city the arts capital of the Prairie Provinces.

Supplementing the arts facilities of the big cities are a number of festivals that attract millions of Canadians each year, and even more American visitors, to other, smaller venues. Some, such as the Banff Festival of the Arts in Alberta, encompass several disciplines; but the two best known, both of them in Ontario, are primarily devoted to theater. The Stratford Festival, set up under the aegis of British director Tyrone Guthrie in 1952, mixes a Shakespearean repertoire with other dramatic classics as well as contemporary plays. By contrast, the Shaw Festival, which takes place in Niagara-on-the-Lake, builds its season around the works of George Bernard Shaw; but the festival also offers various other entertainments, with the emphasis on the relatively light and comic.

But however enthusiastically Cana-

Two men rest beneath an elaborate trompe l'oeil mural painted on the side of a building just off Ottawa's Sparks Street Mall. This traffic-free area, covering five blocks in the heart of the Canadian capital, draws bustling crowds to its shops, department stores, art galleries, and rock gardens.

da's many cultural institutions are patronized, they ultimately owe their continued survival to government assistance. Canada does not have the number of wealthy investors in the entertainment industry that the United States has; so, without government funding, many of the artistic activities that Canadians take for granted simply would not be able to exist.

No institution has been more instrumental in this respect than the Canada Council, which dispenses tens of millions of dollars yearly to support major companies and individual artists, as well as encourages the extension of the arts into all areas of the country. The Canada Council was set up after World War II, and initially its money came from an endowment fund established by inheritance taxes on the estates of two multimillionaires, steel magnate Sir James Dunn and financier I. W. Killam. But within a decade it became clear that, if the arts were to expand successfully in Canada, direct grants to the council from Parliament would be necessary. By the mid-1980s, more than 80 percent of the council's funding came from the government.

The range of activities for which the council may award grants is extensive. A playwright, for example, might apply for a grant of less than $4,000 (Canadian) to help keep body and soul together while completing a work. In contrast, the National Ballet School—the only professional academy of its type in North America, offering both academic and dance education—receives in excess of one million dollars a year from the council's funds.

Another field to benefit from public funding is Canada's film industry. The National Film Board, set up in 1939 and still functioning today, has long been regarded as a model of enlightened government-sponsored film production. Although it made its reputation by financing wartime documentaries and animated films, notably those of the ingenious Norman McLaren, it also funds feature films.

Nonetheless, its restricted budgets could never have sustained a national industry, and out in the commercial world, Canadian feature production languished. In 1966, for example, Canadian filmmakers released only three feature-length works. This dearth of output prompted the government of the day to create the Canadian Film Development Corporation and, for a period, the industry grew by leaps and bounds. Between 1967 and 1978, when the CFDC adopted a new, more commercial orientation, it invested nearly $26 million (Canadian) in more than 220 films with budgets that totaled in excess of $60 million (Canadian).

During this period, some excellent Canadian films were made that received recognition both at home and abroad. Critics started talking about a "Canadian school," exemplified by two low-budget but successful films in both the official languages: Don Shebib's *Going Down the Road*, about two young Maritimers leaving their home and heading for Toronto; and Claude Jutra's *Mon Oncle Antoine*, which concerns a boy growing up in a rural French vil-

lage in the years before World War I.

Other critically acclaimed filmmakers of the time included David Cronenberg, who made a series of low-budget, individualistic horror movies; the veteran Quebecois Gilles Carle, who had a major success with *La Vraie Nature de Bernadette;* Denys Arcand, with *Réjeanne Padovani;* and J. Beaudin, whose simple and affectionate *J.-A. Martin, photographe* was well-liked on the international festival circuit.

Though critically successful, many of the small-budget films of the early 1970s were, however, money-losers,

and pressures grew to reorient the Canadian industry in a more commercial direction. Since then, the emphasis has been on fewer, larger productions with big-name stars, aimed at the international marketplace. *Meatballs, The Apprenticeship of Duddy Kravitz,* and *My American Cousin* were among the biggest money-makers. But the new policy has produced few other commercial successes, let alone artistic ones; and the decline in quality, combined with rising production costs and higher interest rates, has seen the film industry struggling for survival.

Travelers using Montreal's gleaming subway system wait as a train pulls into Peel Street station below the center of the city. Inaugurated in 1966, the metro network comprises three different lines and 58 stations, decorated by Quebec artists and served by silent, rubber-tired trains.

149

5

Some Canadians decry the massive subsidization of the arts, pointing out that the first truly indigenous school of art in the country's history was founded not with the aid of public money, but through the enthusiasm and vision of a circle of painters called the Group of Seven. The beginnings of the movement can be traced back to the meeting between a Toronto doctor, James Mac-Callum, and a young artist named Tom Thomson, in northern Ontario in 1912. MacCallum and Thomson shared a love of the Canadian Far North, and the physician provided moral and financial support to the artist so that he could spend long periods in the wilderness capturing the brilliant colors and haunting landscapes that had been taken for granted by Canadians. Thomson developed his own style, which was disliked by the arbiters of taste in the big cities. Despite the lack of public acceptance, he persevered until the tragic day in 1917 when he drowned on a canoe trip in Ontario's Algonquin Province Park.

By the time of his death, a number of other artists—Lawren Harris, Arthur Lismer, and A. Y. Jackson are today the best remembered—were following Thomson's lead. Eventually the artists totaled seven in number, and they exhibited together. In time, their works became recognized as an authentic Canadian vision; in the 1980s, their canvases were fetching five- and six-figure prices at art sales, as well as occupying a central position in the Canadian collections of Toronto's Ontario Art Gallery and the National Gallery of Canada in Ottawa.

Although the seven are all now dead, a new generation of artists has come forward that still draws its chief inspiration from the land. The haunting magic realism of Alex Colville is nourished by the landscapes of the Maritime Provinces, just as the work of Jack Shadbolt in British Columbia draws its inspirations, as Emily Carr once did, from the gray sea, dark forests, vast mountains, and native Indian culture of the Pacific Coast.

For Canada's Indian and Inuit peoples, the land has always been the greatest source of artistic inspiration; but under the assault of an alien European culture, they lost confidence in their own vision of the world about them. Then, in the 1950s, a growing political awareness led to a rejection of nonnative values and a restatement of faith in their own cultural heritage. Native artists stopped being ashamed of their unique carvings and paintings and found them in considerable demand in the art galleries of Toronto and New York. Purchases of Inuit sculpture at hefty prices, for example, have revived skills threatened with extinction and have added significantly to the income and independence of many families living in the Far North.

The area of cultural endeavor that is perhaps most crucial to Canadians' understanding of themselves is literature. Since World War II, English-language writers have developed a strong tradition in fiction and have finally put an end to the provincial era in Canadian writing, when the only authors known by readers living beyond the nation's frontiers were humorist Stephen Leacock and saga writer Mazo de la Roche.

A transitional figure among the moderns is Morley Callaghan, who followed his literary hero, Ernest Hemingway, to France in the 1920s and wrote amusingly of their encounter in a memoir, *That Summer in Paris.* In a succession of works reflecting his own Roman Catholicism, written after his return to Canada, Callaghan contrasted the world of greed and crime with the spiritual and eternal.

The Canadian novel in its full-fledged form emerged in the works of Hugh MacLennan, described by *The Canadian Encyclopedia* as "the first major English-speaking writer to portray Canada's national character." A Rhodes scholar who had traveled widely in Europe, he tried and failed to complete a novel about his wanderings before discovering his métier nearer home with *Barometer Rising.* The book described the events leading to the Halifax Explosion of 1917, when a munitions carrier blew up in the town's harbor and killed 1,600 people—an event MacLennan himself had survived at the age of 10. Subsequent successes included *Two Solitudes,* covering tensions between the English and French communities in Quebec, and *The Watch That Ends the Night.* Much praised for his descriptive powers, MacLennan encouraged a whole generation of younger writers to have the confidence to address a range of specifically Canadian subject matter.

Another writer of the same generation, whose stature has grown with the passing of time, is Robertson Davies. Born in 1913, the son of a senator, Davies studied at Oxford and dabbled in English theater before returning to Ontario to work for 25 years as editor, then publisher, of the Peterborough *Examiner,* as well as lecturing in literature at the University of Toronto. He also played a role in launching the Stratford Festival. As a novelist, he is best known for two trilogies: the Salterton books, published during the early 1950s, which describe the lives of selected citizens of the fictitious city of

that name, and the Deptford novels, written two decades later and reflecting the author's new-found interest in Jungian psychology.

In a lighter vein, Mordecai Richler gained a reputation as the nation's best satirical writer with the publication, in 1959, of *The Apprenticeship of Duddy Kravitz*. Some of his more recent books, among them *Cocksure* and *St. Urbain's Horseman*, have confirmed his reputation as a writer whose wit and urbanity

rival those of New York authors such as Philip Roth and Joseph Heller.

Female writers feature prominently on the Canadian literary scene. Alice Munro is generally reckoned to be the nation's finest English-language short-story writer, while Margaret Atwood attained a dominant position in the literary world in the 1970s as a promoter of civil-rights causes, feminism, and Canadian nationalism. Poet and critic as well as novelist and essayist, she is prob-

ably best known outside Canada for her novel *Surfacing*, which examines the essential conflict between nature and technology as well as the crucial relationship that exists between Canada and the United States.

In drama, as in other areas of cultural life, Canadians took time to be weaned from second-hand English and American productions. The age of the touring companies ended with World War I, leaving a void of professional

Neil Young, singer-songwriter

Robertson Davies, writer

Leonard Cohen, singer and poet

A GALAXY OF TALENT IN THE CONTEMPORARY ARTS

Canada's heritage in the arts is eclectic and ancient, stretching back to the sophisticated visual culture, based on carving, of the native Indians and Inuit. The French and British brought with them separate traditions in literature and music and two national languages. The contemporary arts scene has grown out of these elements, with a strong input from the United States. As this selection of its best-known talents indicates, the performing arts are now well represented.

Oscar Peterson, jazz pianist

Joni Mitchell, singer-songwriter

Marie-Claire Blais, writer

Lynn Seymour, dancer

Yousuf Karsh, photographer

Mordecai Richler, writer

Donald Sutherland, actor

Geneviève Bujold, actress

Jon Vickers, opera singer

5

theater that took some time to be filled. Between the wars, Canadian theater was characterized by an air of genial amateurism, represented by the Dominion Drama Festival, which had begun in the 1920s to encourage Canadian playwrights and amateur theatrical companies. Each year, it held a festival of finalists in regional drama competitions and gave out awards for best production, best new play, and so forth. The festival died a natural death in the 1970s, by which time dozens of small theaters had established themselves and proved that indigenous drama could compete successfully with imports from Broadway and from London's West End.

The 1970s marked the coming of age of Canadian drama. David French's *Leaving Home*—a grittily realistic play about a young man's coming to terms with his father—made good use of its Newfoundland setting, yet it addressed universal preoccupations. The most controversial play of the 1970s was Michel Tremblay's *Hosanna,* in which a French-Canadian transvestite cries out in rage at the savage dichotomy in his life—a dichotomy that many people took to be symbolic of the division within Canada itself.

Artistically, Quebec has always represented a counterpoint to English Canada, but in the past, it tended to be overshadowed by its partner. Most French writing, for example, was at best a weak reflection of Parisian talents, further handicapped by the small size of the local reading public and the pervasive and inhibiting influence of the Catholic church. Until after World War II, the most widely read novel of French Canada was one written by a visiting Frenchman. Louis Hémon based his *Maria Chapdelaine* on the ex-perience of a year's residence in Montreal and the Lac St. Jean region. The novel reflected a rural, provincial society and glorified its values. Unfortunately, Hémon did not live to see its success; he died at the age of 32, struck by a Canadian Pacific train, before the book was published.

When change did come after the war, the effects were at first felt in painting. There, the Paris connection worked to French Canada's advantage at a time when the French capital was the world leader in the visual arts. The Parisian influence was channeled through two Quebecois, Paul-Émile Borduas and Alfred Pellan, both of whom had studied there between the wars. Otherwise, the two had little in common. While Pellan resolutely avoided identifying his art with any specific school, Borduas developed a movement of his own called "automatism," a style promoting spontaneity above all other artistic criteria. He attracted followers, among them Jean-Paul Riopelle, who subsequently went to Paris and won international renown as a star of the École de Paris group of abstract expressionists.

In literature, the emergence of a distinctive Quebec voice was slower and more gradual. The first breakthrough came in the 1930s, in the work of the poets Alain Gradbois, St. Denys Garneau, and Anne Hébert. Novelist Philippe Panneton, writing under the nom de plume of Ringuet, brought a new note of realism into rural fiction with *Trente Arpents* (Thirty Acres). It was, though, the Quiet Revolution of the 1960s and 1970s that gave French Canada a voice to equal that of the Anglophone section of the nation. In this respect at least, the revolution was strident rather than quiet; the mood among Francophone intellectuals was in part fiercely separatist, a position epitomized by the Montreal review, *Parti pris.* Some writers of the time, including Michel Tremblay, chose to express themselves in the working-class street language *joual.* Others took their chief inspiration from modern French writing but sought to meet the imported product on equal terms. Thus the much-discussed novel by Quebecois writer Marie-Claire Blais, *Une saison dans la vie d'Emmanuel,* triumphantly carried off France's prestigious Prix Médicis in 1966.

To the visitor, the most obvious external signs of Quebec's current cultural vitality are the dinner-theaters and cabarets of Montreal, which provide a showcase for various small theater companies as well as Francophone Canada's most distinctive class of artists, the *chansonniers.* Like their French counterparts, these poet-singers, who often perform their compositions to no accompaniment other than a piano or solo guitar, are much closer to the world of literature than anything in the English folk tradition (except, perhaps, the songs of Anglophone Montrealer Leonard Cohen). Switching easily from love to politics to social satire, they provide a free-ranging commentary on Quebec life, but also on the wider world; some, such as Félix Leclerc, Robert Charlebois, Pauline Julien, and Gilles Vigneault, have gone on to win reputations in French-speaking lands throughout the world.

English-speaking Canada has not seen anything as radical as the Quiet Revolution in its recent history, but in the 1960s it, too, went through a markedly nationalist phase. There were historical events to encourage this development: the approaching centenary of the

154

country's constitutional birth and a growing awareness of Canadian dependence on the United States in matters of defense, industry, and trade. The mood was reflected in the national press and evoked in many different ways—from demands for controls over land acquisition by nonresidents to claims on the university campuses that Canadians take precedence over Americans in teaching positions.

The nationalist era made positive contributions to Canada's perception of itself but, at the same time, isolated once again the fact that, to be positive about Canada, many Canadians feel moved to be negative about the United States. The love-hate relationship between Canada and the United States may not be entirely healthy, but geography and history have decreed that there is no escaping it. One of the positive aspects of the relationship is that, by forcing Canadians to explore their own world view, it has invested Canadian literature, art, and drama with most of its uniqueness. Not a startling claim, perhaps, but then Canadians are a modest people who can even laugh at the charge that they have much to be modest about. They were not always able to do that, and this change alone is a measure of the increased confidence and achievement that have marked Canada's development during the second half of the 20th century. □

ACKNOWLEDGMENTS

The index for this book was prepared by Vicki Robinson. For their help in the preparation of this volume, the editors also wish to thank the following: Joseph Agnew, Canadian Recreational Canoeing Association, Hyde Park, Ontario; Eileen Argyris, Colborne Chronicle, Colborne, Ontario ; Moira Banks, London; Mike Brown, London; Kate Cann, Guildford, Surrey, England; W. A. Chestnut, Colborne, Ontario; Windsor Chorlton, London; Colborne Fire Department, Colborne, Ontario; Geoff Crew, Office of the Inspector General of Banks, Ottawa; Leigh Drushka, Toronto; Janet Farmer, Canadian High Commission, London; Jean-Paul Fontaine, Société d'Énergie de la Baie James, Montreal; Alex Harnden, Ottawa; R. S. Harnett, Council of Forest Industries of British Columbia, London; Alison Hart, Vancouver, B.C. ; Barbara Moir Hicks, London; J. A. Hillier, British Geological Survey, London; H. Hirschel, Stuttgart; Ann House, Canadian High Commission, London; Joanna Hucker, London; Jeanne Johnson, London; Robert Keir, Ministry of Tourism and Recreation, Ontario; Elizabeth Ketchum, Canadian High Commission, London; Yadira and Wally Krul, Ottawa; Wayne Laco, Winnipeg, Manitoba; Wency Laywine, Ontario Tourism, London; Jonathan Lemco, SAIS, Johns Hopkins University, Washington, D.C.; Elizabeth MacCallum, London; Alex McDonald, Colborne, Ontario; Sally Mitchell, Province of Nova Scotia, London; Ken Murdock, Winnipeg, Manitoba; Judith Paradis-Pastori, Délégation Générale du Québec, London; Ruth Parkhouse, Hudson's Bay Company, London; Shirley Parrott, British Columbia Government, London; Elizabeth Plint, Oxford, England; Police Station, Terrace Bay, Ontario; Jayne E. Rohrich, Alexandria, Virginia; Heather Roskey, Government of Alberta, London; Sally Rowland, Saffron Walden, Essex, England; William Russell, Canadian High Commission, London; Saskatchewan Government, London; W. Dieter Scharf, Toronto; Huguette Schwartz, Quebec; Jasmine Spencer, London; Eliza Staples, Ottawa; Colette Stockum, Alexandria, Virginia; Rosanne Teal, Colborne, Ontario; Deborah Thompson, London; Arvid Thorstensen, Council of Forest Industries of British Columbia, Vancouver, B.C.; P. Viererbl, Stuttgart; Carol Woo, The Canadian Encyclopedia, Edmonton, Alberta; Ann Young, Ottawa; Esther A. Zeller, Toronto.

PICTURE CREDITS

Credits from left to right are separated by semicolons, from top to bottom by dashes.

Cover: Hans Wiesenhofer, Pöllau, Austria. Front endpaper: Map by Roger Stewart, London. Back endpaper: Digitized map by Ralph Scott/Chapman Bounford, London.

1, 2: © Flag Research Center, Winchester, Massachusetts. 6, 7: Hans Wiesenhofer, Pöllau, Austria, map by Ralph Scott/Chapman Bounford, London. 8, 9: Gary Hershorn, © Day in The Life of Canada/Colorific!, London. 10, 11: Karl-Heinz Raach, Freiburg, Germany. 12, 13: Karl-Heinz Raach, Freiburg, Germany, map by Ralph Scott/Chapman Bounford, London. 14, 15: Hans Wiesenhofer, Pöllau, Austria. 16, 17: Karl-Heinz Raach, Freiburg, Germany. 18: Mike Yamashita from Colorific!, London. 19: Map by Ralph Scott/Chapman Bounford, London. 20: Michael Freeman, London. 21: R. Hamaguchi from Image Finders Photo Agency, Vancouver, B.C., Canada. 22-24: Michael Freeman, London. 25: P. Hinous from Agence Top, Paris. 27: J. A. Kraulis from Masterfile, Toronto. 28, 29: Pierre Toutain, Paris. 30, 31: Harald Sund, Seattle, Washington. 32, 33: Stephanie Maze from Woodfin Camp Inc., Washington, D.C. 34: Ottmar Bierwagen, Toronto. 35: Brian Milne from First Light, Toronto. 36, 37: Hans Wiesenhofer, Pöllau, Austria. 38: Karl-Heinz Raach, Freiburg, Germany. 39: Brian Milne from First Light, Toronto. 40-49: Hans Wiesenhofer, Pöllau, Austria (insets: 40, top left: Bernard Martin from Alpine Diffusion, Montreal; bottom left: Alan Kemp from Image Finders Photo Agency, Vancouver, B.C., Canada; 42, bottom right: Michel Faugère from Alpha Diffusion, Montreal; 45, top left and right: Michael Freeman, London; bottom: Harald Mante, Dortmund, Germany; 48, top and center: Karl-Heinz Raach, Freiburg, Germany; bottom left: Douglas Leighton, Banff, Alberta, Canada. 50, 51: Print by William Richards, Collection Hudson's Bay Company, Winnipeg, Manitoba, Canada, photo Michael Holford, Loughton, Essex, England. 52, 53: Anonymous "Vallard Atlas" map, 1547, courtesy The Huntington Library, San Marino, California. 54: Illustration from *Les Voyages du Sieur de Champlain*, 1613, courtesy The Houghton Library, Harvard University, Cambridge, Massachusetts. 55: Illustration from *Les Voyages du Sieur de Champlain*, 1613, photo BBC Hulton Picture Library, London. 56: Mid-19th-century lithograph by George Catlin, Mansell Collection, London. 57: Musée du Seminaire de Québec, photo Pierre Soulard. 58, 59: Colored engraving by J. and C. Bowles, 1797, photo E. T. Archive, London. 61: Lithograph by H. A. Strong, Glenbow Archives, Calgary, Alberta, Canada. 62: Engraving by S. Freeman from a drawing by Thomas Hamel after the original picture at St. Malo, photo BBC Hulton Picture Library, London; Hudson's Bay Company, Winnipeg, Manitoba, Canada—Engraving by W. Say after a drawing by John Ross, photo Mary Evans Picture Library, London. 63: Mansell Collection, London; Michael Freeman, London. 64: Colored lithograph by H. Jones after a watercolor by Peter Rindisbacher, courtesy Picture Division, Public Archives of Canada, Ottawa. 65: Provincial Archives of Alberta, Edmonton, Alberta, Canada, Ernest Brown Collection. 66: E. A. Hegg, courtesy Special Collections Division, University of Washington Libraries, Seattle, Washington. 67: Provincial Archives of Alberta, Edmonton, Alberta, Canada, Ernest Brown Collection—Popperfoto, London. 68: Painting by Robert Bradford, courtesy National Aviation Museum, Ottawa. 69: Provincial Archives of Manitoba, Winnipeg, Manitoba, Canada, Foote Collection. 70: Courtesy Punch Publications, London. 71: Dilip Mehta, Contact/Colorific!, London. 72, 73: BBC Hulton Picture Library, London, Department of Public Relations, Canadian Pacific, London. 74, 75: Provincial Archives of Manitoba, Winnipeg, Manitoba, Canada, Boundary Commission Collection; Saskatchewan Archives Board, Regina, Saskatchewan, Canada—Glenbow Archives, Calgary, Alberta, Canada. 76, 77: Glenbow Archives, Calgary, Alberta, Canada—Royal Commonwealth Society Library, A. H. Fisher Collection, Provincial Archives of Alberta, Edmonton, Alberta, Canada, Ernest Brown Collection. 78, 79: Glenbow Archives, Calgary, Alberta, Canada. 80: Hans Wiesenhofer, Pöllau, Austria; Karl-Heinz Raach, Freiburg, Germany—Hans Wiesenhofer, Pöllau, Austria—Scott Rowed, Banff, Alberta, Canada; Hans Wiesenhofer, Pöllau, Austria. 81: Hans Wiesenhofer, Pöllau, Austria—Pierre Toutain, Paris. 82: Gerd Ludwig from Visum, Hamburg. 83: Harald Mante, Dortmund, Germany. 85, 86: Michael Freeman, London. 89: Hans Blohm from Masterfile, Toronto. 90, 91: Ottmar Bierwagen, Toronto (2)—Thomas Nebbia from Woodfin Camp Inc., Washington, D.C. 92, 93: Michael Freeman, London. 94: Derek Caron from Masterfile, Toronto. 95: Michael Freeman, London. 96, 97: Hans Wiesenhofer, Pöllau, Austria. 98-101: Karl-Heinz Raach, Freiburg, Germany. 102: Hans Wiesenhofer, Pöllau, Austria. 104, 105: Coats of arms courtesy the Picture Division, Public Archives Canada, Ottawa. Chart by Ralph Scott/Chapman Bounford, London. 106: Harald Mante, Dortmund, Germany. 107: Canadian Pacific Corporate Archives, Montreal. 108: Canadair Ltd., Montreal. 109: Arthur Schatz, New York. 111: Ottmar Bierwagen, Toronto. 112: Hans Wiesenhofer, Pöllau, Austria. 114: J. M. Petit from Alpha Diffusion, Montreal—Hydro-Quebec, Quebec City. 115: Ottmar Bierwagen, Toronto—Wolfgang Steche from Visum, Hamburg. 116, 117: Karl-Heinz Raach, Freiburg, Germany. 118: Pierre Toutain, Paris. 119: P. E. I. Potato Commodity Marketing Board, Charlottetown, Prince Edward Island, Canada. 120, 121: Harald Mante, Dortmund, Germany. 122, 123: Hans Wiesenhofer, Pöllau, Austria. 124: B. Truncik from Photo/Graphics, Vancouver, B.C., Canada; Edward Dossetter, courtesy Department Library Services, American Museum of Natural History, New York. 125: B. Truncik from Photo/Graphics, Vancouver, B.C., Canada. 126, 127: Werner Forman Archive, London, courtesy Museum of Anthropology, University of British Columbia; Werner Forman Archive, London, courtesy National Museum of Man, Ottawa; Werner Forman Archive, London, courtesy Provincial Museum, British Columbia—Werner Forman Archive, London, courtesy Cape Masset Collection, Provincial Museum, British Columbia; Werner Forman Archive, London, courtesy The British Museum. 128, 129: Werner Forman Archive, London, courtesy Museum of Anthropology, University of British Columbia; Werner Forman Archive, London, courtesy McCord Museum, Montreal—Werner Forman Archive, London, courtesy National Museum of Man, Ottawa. 130, 131: Werner Forman Archive, London, courtesy James Hooper Collection—Werner Forman Archive, London, Provincial Museum, British Columbia; Werner Forman Archive, London, courtesy Mr. and Mrs. M. I. Sosland. 132, 133: Pierre Toutain, Paris. 134: Douglas Leighton, Banff, Alberta, Canada. 135: Gerd Ludwig from Visum, Hamburg. 136, 137: J. A. Kraulis from Masterfile, Toronto. 138: Terry Hancey from Masterfile, Toronto. 140, 141: Scott Rowed, Banff, Alberta, Canada. 142: Ted Grant from Masterfile,Toronto—I. Media from Masterfile, Toronto—Sherman Hines from Masterfile, Toronto. 143: Bill Brooks from Masterfile, Toronto—Francis Lepine from Valan Photos, Montreal—Janet F. Dwyer from First Light, Toronto. 144, 145: Michael Freeman, London. 147: Koos Dykstra from Image Finders Photo Agency, Vancouver, B.C., Canada. 148, 149: Michael Freeman, London. 151: Hans Wiesenhofer, Pöllau, Austria. 152: Camera Press, London; Penguin Books, London—Pieter van Acker from Camera Press, London—David Redfern, London; Camera Press, London. 153: Canapress Photo Service, Toronto (2); Tara Heinemann from Camera Press, London—Malak from Camera Press, London—Terry O'Neill from Camera Press, London; The Kobal Collection, London; Clive Barda, London. 155: Oil on canvas, Art Gallery of Ontario, Toronto, courtesy Mrs. James H. Knox, Vancouver, B.C., Canada, and Lawren P. Harris, Ottawa.

BIBLIOGRAPHY

BOOKS

Anderson, Allan, and Betty Tomlinson, *Greetings from Canada*. Toronto: Macmillan of Canada, 1978.

Artibise, Alan, *Winnipeg: An Illustrated History*. Toronto: James Lorimer & Company, 1977.

Berton, Pierre:
Klondike: The Last Great Goldrush. Toronto: McClelland and Stewart, 1972.
The Klondike Quest. Toronto: McClelland and Stewart, 1983.

Bothwell, Robert, Ian Drummond, and John English, *Canada Since 1945*. Toronto: University of Toronto Press, 1981.

Brebner, J. Bartlett, *Canada*. Ann Arbor, Michigan: The University of Michigan Press, 1960.

Canada Handbook. Ottawa: Minister of Supply and Services Canada, 1984.

The Canadian Encyclopedia. Edmonton: Hurtig Publishers, 1985.

Careless, J. M. S., ed., *Colonists and Canadians 1760-1867*. Toronto: Macmillan of Canada, 1971.

Charon, Milly, ed., *Between Two Worlds: The Canadian Immigration Experience*. Dunvegan, Canada: Quadrant Editions, 1983.

Creighton, Donald, *The Story of Canada*. London: Faber and Faber, 1965.

Elliot, Jean Leonard, ed., *Two Nations, Many Cultures*. Scarborough, Canada: Prentice-Hall, 1983.

Epp, H. Frank, *Mennonites in Canada*. Toronto: Macmillan of Canada, 1974.

Fodor's Canada. London: Hodder and Stoughton, 1985.

Fowke, V., *Canadian Agricultural Policy*. Toronto: University of Toronto Press, 1946.

Fulford, Robert, *An Introduction to the Arts in Canada*. Toronto: Copp Clark Publishing, 1977.

Fulford, Robert, David Godfrey, and Abraham Rotstein, eds., *Read Canadian*. Toronto: James Lewis and Samuel, 1972.

Gray, James H., *Boomtime*. Toronto: Western Producer Prairie Books, 1979.

Gwyn, Richard, *The 49th Paradox*. Toronto: McClelland and Stewart, 1985.

Hall, Gerry, *Offbeat Canada*. Scarborough, Canada: New American Library of Canada Limited, 1981.

Hawthorn, A., *Art of the Kwakiutl Indians*. Vancouver: University of British Columbia, 1967.

Higgs, David, *The Portuguese in Canada*. Ottawa: Canadian Historical Association, 1965.

Hill, Douglas, *The Opening of the Canadian West*. London: Heinemann, 1967.

Holm, Bill, *N.W. Coast Indian Art: An Analysis of Form*. Vancouver: Douglas McIntyre, 1975.

Johnson, Hugh, *The East Indians in Canada*. Ottawa: Canadian Historical Association, 1984.

Kesterton, W. H., *A History of Journalism in Canada*. Toronto: McClelland and Stewart, 1970.

Kilbourn, William, ed., *Canada: A Guide to the Peaceable Kingdom*. Toronto: Macmillan of Canada, 1970.

King, J. C. H., *Portrait Masks from N.W. Coast of America*. London: Thames and Hudson, 1979.

Kostash, Myrna, *All of Baba's Children*. Edmonton: Hertig Publishers, 1977.

Kurelek, William, *A Prairie Boy's Winter and Summer*. Montreal: Tundra Books, 1978.

Leacock, Stephen, *Canada: The Foundations of Its Future*. Montreal: The House of Seagram, 1941.

Lehane, Brendan, *The Northwest Passage* (The Seafarers series). Alexandria, Virginia: Time-Life Books, 1981.

Lindstorm-Best, Varpu, *The Finns in Canada*. Ottawa: Canadian Historical Association, 1985.

MacKay, Douglas, *The Honourable Company: A History of the Hudson's Bay Company*. Toronto: McClelland and Stewart, 1949.

McNaught, Kenneth, *The Pelican History of Canada*. Harmondsworth, England: Penguin Books, 1985.

Mason, Bill, *Path of the Paddle*. Toronto: Van Nostrand Reinhold, 1980.

Newman, Peter C.:
The Acquisitors. Toronto: Seal Books, 1982. *The Canadian Establishment*. Toronto: Seal Books, 1983. *Company of Adventurers*. Ontario: Penguin Books, 1985.
Flame of Power. Toronto: McClelland and Stewart, 1965.

Orkin, M. Mark, and Isaac Bickerstaff, *Canajah, Eh?* Toronto: General Publishing, 1982.

Petrie, J. Francis, *Roll out the Barrel*. Erin, Canada: Boston Mills Press, 1985.

Robertson, H., *Salt of the Earth*. Toronto: J. Lorimer, 1974.

Sinclair, Andrew, ed., *Jack London: The Call of the Wild, White Fang, and Other Stories*. Harmondsworth, England: Penguin Books, 1985.

Stanley, G. F. G., *Louis Riel: Patriot or Rebel?* Ottawa: Canadian Historical Association, 1954.

Tanner, Ogden, and the Editors of Time-Life Books, *The Canadians*. (The Old West series). Alexandria, Virginia: Time-Life Books, 1977.

Whalley, John:
Canadian Trade Policies and the World Economy. Toronto: University of Toronto Press, 1985. *Canada-United States Free Trade*. Toronto: University of Toronto Press, 1985.

Woodcock, G., and I. Avakumovic, *The Doukhobors*. Toronto: Oxford University Press, 1968.

Woodcock, George, *Canada and the Canadians*. London: Faber and Faber, 1970.

PERIODICALS

"Black September," *Saturday Night*, February 1986.

"Bonjour to Trudeau's Bilingual Provinces," *The Guardian*, August 11, 1983.

"Canada: A Survey," *The Economist*, August 7, 1982.

"Calgary, Canada's Not So Wild West," *National Geographic*, March 1984.

"Call of the North, Yukon Fever," *National Geographic*, April 1978.

"Canada: Fin?" *The Economist*, June 15, 1985.

"Canada's Highway to the Sea," *National Geographic*, May 1980.

"Canada Survey," *Financial Times*, July 5, 1985.

"Canadian Energy: Head West Again," *The Economist*, August 3, 1985.

"Heart of the Canadian Rockies," *National Geographic*, June 1980.

"How Canadians Lose at the Polls," *Maclean's*, August 13, 1984.

"Measuring Ottawa's Fat," *Western Report*, March 24, 1986.

"The Most Influential Private Citizen in Canada," *Saturday Night*, July 1984.

"Mulroney Takes Command," *Maclean's*, October 1, 1984.

"Newfoundland, the Enduring Rock," *National Geographic*, May 1986.

"The Northern Lights," *Sunday Times*, December 12, 1976.

"Ottawa's Season of Secrecy," *Maclean's*, November 5, 1984.

"Parti Québécois Elects New Leader and Steps Away from Separatism," *The Times*, October 1, 1985.

"The Power and the Glory in Quebec," *Geo*, December 1979.

"Racism without Colour: The Catholic Ethic and Ethnicity in Quebec," *Race and Class*, summer 1983.

"A Rancorous Finale," *Maclean's*, December 30, 1985.

"A 'Ready' Mulroney Watched," *Maclean's*, June 25, 1984.

"Sitting Duck," *Saturday Night*, August 1985.

"Timid New World: A Survey of Canada," *The Economist*, February 15, 1986.

"Tory Problems in Quebec," *Maclean's*, January 20, 1986.

"Tough Talk and Temerity," *Maclean's*, December 9, 1985.

"The Trials of Transition," *Saturday Night*, April 1985.

"The Unlikely Godfather," *Saturday Night*, May 1985.

INDEX

Numbers in italics refer to an illustration of the subject mentioned.

Time-Life Books Inc. offers a wide range of fine recordings, including a *Rock 'n' Roll Era* series. For subscription information, call 1-800-621-7026, or write Time-Life Music, P.O. Box C-32068, Richmond, Virginia 23261-2068.